MAKING MONEY

EDWARD C. ROCHETTE

To counterfeit is DEATH
New Jersey - 1756

RENAISSANCE
HOUSE PUBLISHERS

Most of this work is original. Some stories are columns that have appeared in *COINage* magazine, *Numismatic News,* or were syndicated through the Los Angeles Times Syndicate. Those are reprinted with permission.

Renaissance House
A Division of JENDE-HAGAN, INC.
541 Oak Street • P.O. Box 177
Frederick, CO   80530

Library of Congress Cataloging in Publication Data

Rochette, Edward C., 1927–
   Making money.

   Includes index.
   1. Counterfeits and counterfeiting--History.
2. Money--History. I. Title.
HG335.R63   1986   364.1'33'09   86-22120
ISBN 0-939650-25-8 (pbk.)

OTHER BOOKS BY THE AUTHOR

MEDALLIC PORTRAITS OF JOHN F. KENNEDY

COINS QUESTIONS AND ANSWERS
(Co-author, first edition)

A COIN COLLECTORS' SELECTION OF COINTOONS
(Editor)

THE OTHER SIDE OF THE COIN

This book is for M.A.

INTRODUCTION

Riches! The dream of rogues and rascals! Some dream big and live their dreams, albeit briefly. These are not necessarily nice dreams, but I must confess grudging admiration. I find the tales of monetary chicanery intriguing. I find myself relating to dreamers with kingdoms of their own, tolerating those with visions of untold wealth, thanks to their private mints. However, as with all dreams, there comes a time to awaken and face reality.

I find adventure in peering over the shoulders of the dreamers, the schemers, and the counterfeiters. It has been fun rescuing the would-be emperors from obscurity. Although a few tales have been told and retold, these have, for the most part, been lost in forgotten newspaper files and historic archives.

These stories are true. Most come from the past, for today few coins are counterfeited for reasons of commerce Admittedly, some scarce and rare coins are now being created to satisfy the collector's urge. Now, too, would-be kingdom makers are ridiculed. rather than humored.

The collecting of counterfeit coin and currency, if one is to follow the letter of the law, is illegal. However, researching and reading about them is not. I have had the enjoyment of research. I hope you have the fun of reading.

E.C.R.

FOREWORD

Money talks. Sure, that's an old expression, perhaps rather trite, but it is true. Money not only talks, it is an excellent story teller.

So is Ed Rochette. Combine the two and you've got interesting conversation, and in the case of this book. interesting reading.

Too many of us, though, have not stopped to "listen" to the stories money has to tell. Many people continually think about ways to earn money—or otherwise acquire significant quantities of it. But most of us probably view what's in our pocketbooks like a utility the same way we take electricity for granted: we flip a switch and the light goes on.

We take it for granted that our pocket change and our paper money are genuine, still worth face value, and readily redeemable for chewing gum, bus fare, or a pair of first base seats for that big double-header.

Yet there are so many other ways our money could be talking to us. In his earlier book, *The Other Side of the Coin*, Ed Rochette presented many fascinating stories about the art, the history, and the romance of coins and currency. Each coin or bill, no matter how worn or tattered, had a tale to tell.

In this equally delightful book, Ed colorfully describes the legal and illegal production of money and how money has played a critical and sometimes comical role in history.

These stories will give you a new perspective on your common pocket change. You'll realize there is really nothing common about it at all.

And after you've become good friends with those loose coins and creased paper bills, after you've stopped taking them for granted, only to buy groceries or tip the doorman, then you'll always be ready to listen to the astounding stories money has to tell.

Money talks, but you've got to listen.

--Donn Pearlman
Coin Collectors' Corner
WBBM—CBS, Chicago

CONTENTS

UNCOMMON TALES OF COMMON COUNTERFEITERS—Part I

UNCOMMON TALES OF COMMON COUNTERFEITERS — Part II

THE CLASSIC TALES

THE COUNTERFEITERS PLOT TO KIDNAP LINCOLN'S BODY!

The plot was pure Agatha Christie, Alfred Hitchcock, even A. Conan Doyle, rolled into one great mystery. But it also had a twist of Mack Sennett's Keystone Cops, and that was the story's undoing. If the intent had not been so profane, such an insult to the American intellect, the public might have found some humor in the antics of the perpetrators. Instead, the public was incensed. The incident has long been forgotten, but it was all there to read on the front page of the Saturday morning, November 14, 1876, edition of the *Chicago Daily Tribune*. An attempt had been made to kidnap the body of Abraham Lincoln and hold it for ransom—the price being the release of a man who could make paper money almost as good as the government.

Ben Boyd was a master engraver and plate engraver. His work earned him the admiration of a certain group and the security of a decade-long term at the federal penitentiary at Joliet, Illinois. Boyd's skills had been the mainstay employment of a group of *koniakers*, who in turn supplied *shovers* with an imitation of U.S. currency of such quality that it readily circulated throughout the Midwest-- from Minnesota to Texas. Treasury officials failed to appreciate Boyd's skills and took a dim view of this active competition with the Bureau of Engraving and Printing's monopoly on the production of legal tender; but Boyd's friends found him indispensable. Others who could imitate Boyd's work were also incarcerated and the period around our nation's centennial caused the Secret Service little concern on the subject of spurious notes. To end their period of

unemployment and return to their more affluent lifestyle, Boyd's associates decided to secure his immediate release. They were aware that no amount of money, real or otherwise, could buy a pardon for him. But what if they had something to trade for Boyd—say, the body of Abraham Lincoln? Even though the President had been dead over eleven years, his body had not yet been assigned a final resting place.

A grubby tavern called "The Hub," at 294 West Madison in downtown Chicago, was selected as plot head- quarters. It was not a clever choice. The Hub had long been suspected as a meeting place for counterfeiters and was under constant surveillance by the Secret Service. Louis C. Swegles, one of the tavern's habitues, was a government informer. Boyish in appearance and thought too young to be taken seriously, Swegles found it easy to join in various conversations. He allowed himself to be "talked into" joining the plot to kidnap Lincoln's remains. Other conspirators included the tavern's owner, Jack Mullins; Jack Hughes, a passer of Boyd's currency; and Herbert Nelson, who was to drive the wagon needed to haul Lincoln's body. Swegles kept the Secret Service informed of developments. The agency in turn hired Pinkerton detectives to supple- ment their force, thus introducing the Keystone element to the story.

The evening of November 7, 1876, was selected as the night to steal Lincoln's body from its white marble sarcophagus in Springfield's Oak Ridge Cemetery. It was election night in the Illinois capital and undoubtedly the citizenry would be too preoccupied to concern themselves with possible graveside activities. Public and private detectives preceded the kidnap gang to the gravesite by hours and the long, cold wait took its toll. One of the rental cops caught a numb finger in the trigger guard of his service revolver. He yanked, the gun fired, and the conspirators fled. A pitched gun battle ensued and for several minutes the Secret Servicemen were pinned down—by the Pinkertons! The foiled kidnappers were well on their way back to Chicago before those exchanging shots realized that they were both on the same side.

When the gang regrouped several days later at The Hub, government agents were waiting—this time without the help of Pinkerton's. Instead of securing Ben Boyd's release, the conspirators too were imprisoned. Ironically, a number of their friends were convicted in a later conspiracy to free them all from jail. But for a short time, at least, counterfeit currency was not the problem that it had once been for midwestern merchants—Secret Service had done its job.

Carl Wilhelm Becker

THE TALE OF THE TWO BECKERS

CARL WILHELM BECKER
1772-1830

When coin collecting was considered the hobby of royalty, and the price of desired specimens mere assessments against royal treasuries, there were certain dealers whose livelihood depended on filling the want lists of sovereign collectors. The bankers Rothschild in Frankfurt, William Foster in London, T.E. Mionnet in Paris, were among them. Herr Carl Wilhelm Becker, sometimes of Munich, supplied ancient Greek, Roman and Medieval coins to kings, princes and counts, to government museums, to curators of regal collections, and to prominent numismatists of the day. The coins were mostly of his own manufacture.

That Carl Becker was an artist cannot be disputed. He prepared his dies and coins in an era that preceded the modern means of mechanical reproduction. Becker cut his dies by hand, copying them from genuine pieces passing through his studio or from coins viewed in museums or collections he studied.

Becker's beginnings in the commercial world were not as a forger of coins; he had inherited a wine business from his father. When this failed, he became a draper. The second enterprise met the fate of the first. The year: 1803. Becker had always harbored ambitions to be a sculptor and this was as good a time as any to pursue that dream. He became a student engraver at the Royal Mint of Bavaria in Munich.

Years later, when asked why he turned his talents to making imitations of ancient coins, he referred to this early period at the mint, claiming that a wealthy Bavarian baron sold him a gold coin of Emperor Commodus. Discovering it to be a counterfeit, Becker returned the coin to the baron only to find himself severely chastised by the baron for meddling in an area he did not understand. Becker got his revenge by creating a false piece intentionally prepared for sale to the baron. It was so easy that the young engraver just continued making copies, many of which ended up in the prominent museums of Europe.

Becker kept meticulous records, inventorying the spurious pieces of his manufacture. In all, he made dies for approximately 340 different coins and medals. Audaciously he once ventured to Vienna to offer all his dies for sale to the emperor. "How else could anyone detect my false coins if they could not compare them to my dies," he asked?

Becker was unsuccessful in selling his dies, not because of a lack of interest in the offer but for the more mundane reason that his price was too high. In 1911, 81 years after Becker's death, most of his dies came under the control of the Kaiser Friedrich Museum in Berlin. Soft metal impressions were made from the dies and distributed to all prominent museums in Europe. The collections were examined, the counterfeits culled, but not disposed of. Today, Becker counterfeits are considered respectable and collectible. What better tribute could be paid to the wine merchant and draper who always wanted to be an artist?

CHARLES "SCRATCH" BECKER
1847-1916

Charles Becker was to authorities on both sides of the Atlantic as Carl

Charles "Scratch" Becker

Becker was to museum curators, princes and barons: an expert forger and a cause of real concern. Herr Charles Becker concentrated on the monetary instruments of the day; Herr Carl Becker on ancient coins of Greece and Rome. Both gained the grudging admiration of their adversaries and, although they lived almost a century apart, their lives drew curious parallels.

Both Beckers learned their engraving skills in Germany. Carl concentrated on coins, Charles on paper money. Both were good enough to fool experts. William Pinkerton, son of the founder of the great detective agency, gave the latter Becker an off-hand compliment when he said, "A bogus banknote, drawn by Becker's steady hand, could undergo microscopic scrutiny and still remain undetected." An exaggeration perhaps, but a definite compliment. Becker's steady hand earned him the nickname, "Scratch."

Scratch Becker's work did not always go undetected. In 1872 he

4

learned first-hand the living conditions inside the dark, damp Turkish prison at Smyrna. He and several companions were caught flooding Turkey with cleverly forged sight drafts. Prison life was not to his liking and Becker escaped, making his way to the United States via London. En route, he continued to make the paper to pay his way.

Five years later, in 1877, Becker faced a judge again. Arrested on forgery charges, he escaped a prison term by turning state's evidence. Freedom was not to run long. Involved with a counterfeit group operating in Europe, Becker was charged with the manufacture of bogus 1,000-franc notes of the Bank of France. This caper earned him a six and one-half-year holiday in the penitentiary.

Becker's last incarceration was a three-year stretch in San Quentin for producing bogus U.S. Treasury currency notes. Whether he was born again, or just plain tired at age 56, Becker announced he was putting down his pen on his release in 1903.

Scratch Becker decided to capitalize on name recognition with U.S. bankers and for a short period produced and marketed an "ineradicable" ink that would defy any forger's attempt to tamper with it. This enterprise failed. Seeking permanent roots, Becker purchased a little house on Etna Street on New York's East Side. His last years were spent operating a saloon in Brooklyn and telling his story to any patron willing to listen. Far from modest or contrite, Becker liked to compare himself to Benvenuto Cellini, the famed sculptor of the Italian Renaissance. Had he known about Carl Wilhelm Becker, he would have undoubtedly compared himself with him, too. They had so much in common.

ANOTHER BECKER?

In the early 1960's, a firm calling itself Becker Reproductions operated in the Bronx, on 156 Street. Whether there was a third Becker in the field of replication, or the firm intended to capitalize on collector recognition of the name, is not known. The company produced a series of imitation ancient coins for "the collector who could not afford the original." Ironically, neither could Becker Reproductions. They copied some counterfeits.

The Becker replicas were copies of the masterpieces of ancient Greek and Roman coins in the collection of the British Museum. The museum has long made electrocopies of the choice specimens in its collections for research and study by numismatic scholars and for display in other museums. Becker Reproductions obtained a set of the study copies and made cast copies of its own. There was no intent to deceive; each of the modern Becker's ancient coins was edge marked, COPY!

THE CASE AGAINST REVEREND MR. SMITH

Jamaica in 1774 was a British colony, and the laws and customs of Great Britain prevailed. Punishment for counterfeiting at the time was DEATH! The evidence against Rev. Francis Smith was largely circumstantial and, through later numismatic research, found to be flawed. The Crown prosecutors, unaware of the strategies of the colonial mintmasters for the King of Spain, based their case on the design of the coins entered into evidence. The Reverend Smith was guilty of a crime, but not one serious enough to warrant death.

The young curate from England fell madly in love with the daughter of a city merchant. She was fair, beautiful, and equally in love with Francis Smith. But for the times, it was an affair that could never be—through her veins flowed the blood of a slave forebear. The two kept their liaison secret and when the girl became pregnant, no one suspected the clergyman.

The city merchant idolized his daughter and was grief-striken by her adamant refusal to name her lover. His paternal pride was shattered and his response was—suicide! As was customary since he was deeply in debt, the father's estate and personal effects, daughter included because of her blood, were to be sold at public auction.

One can appreciate the young curate's desperate thoughts, even understand his "solution" to the problem. He would attend the auction and buy his sweetheart and his yet unborn child. The financial situation of the young priest is not known, but shortly before the auction, he passed a gold coin unfamiliar in design to those who dealt in currency in the capital city of Kingston. Someone deemed it counterfeit and the Reverend Smith was arrested.

An account of the situation appeared much later in a Jamaican newspaper, the *St. Jago de la Vega Gazette*, dated December 19, 1801:

> A number of counterfeit doubloons and Eight-Dollar pieces are now in circulation. The inscription on the face is Carol's 3d., date 1761. The face does not by any means resemble any effigy given of him on any coins issued by the Spanish government during his reign. It is a perfect copy of the head of Ferdinand the 6th, which appears on the doubloons issued by him ten years before the accession of Charles the 3rd to the

throne. The pieces now in circulation are said to have been coined by Reverend Mr. Smith, who suffered for the crime many years ago on the Kingston Parade.

Court records in Kingston confirm that in April 1775, the case of the King against the Reverend Francis Smith was heard and a verdict of "guilty" rendered. If the case were based solely on the evidence later reported in the press, there appears to have been a serious miscarriage of justice. Such evidence can only create reasonable doubt as to the Reverend Smith's guilt.

As documented in the standard reference *Las Monedas Espanolas*, by Juan R. Cayon and Carlos Castan, when Ferdinand VI died and Charles III ascended the throne of Spain, not all colonial mint engravers knew what the new king looked like. Several engravers therefore used the portrait of the old with the legends of the new. The 1761 eight-escudo gold piece called a doubloon is one such example.

Many legends have a happy ending and the story of Reverend Smith is no exception. Smith's sweetheart did mount the auction block and commanded a large sum. Her master was a benevolent merchant and she became a "lady of fashion and stature." The child born to her shortly after Smith's execution was a girl who grew up to be more beautiful than her mother and married a young English nobleman. Their union was the beginning of one of today's most prominent English families. While the story has been embellished through the generations, Rev. Francis Smith was nevertheless tried, found guilty and executed. The evidence was based on a coin that may well have been, as the issuers intended, genuine currency of the colonial empire of the King of Spain.

A Spanish colonial eight-escudo gold piece dated 1761 with the portrait of

Ferdinand VI and the legends of Charles III

A CASE FROM SHERLOCK HOLMES

LONDON, May 13, 1982—The weather is a disappointment. No cold, wet drizzle or pea-soup fog, just unseasonably bright, sunshiny weather and a prohibition on sooty, soft coal burning fireplaces. Missing, too, is a most famous address—221B Baker Street. In its place is a large office building numbered 215-230. Fortunately, reality will not stand in the way of a vivid imagination.

I head for 221B Baker Street much as Dr. John B. Watson did nearly a century earlier—by cab. Dr. Watson's companion that day in 1889 was Victor Hatherly, a hydraulic engineer; my companion is the vivid imagination.

Overlooking the absence of 221B I eavesdrop on Sherlock Holmes' *Adventure of the Engineer's Thumb*. Victor Hatherly is the engineer, a young man, not over twenty-five. His face reflects the shock and terrifying experience of the night before. Hatherly's left hand bears fresh bandages. Dr. Watson has just attended to an amputated thumb and together they have come to Holmes'

lodgings. Hatherly begins his story, "Yesterday a man offered me fifty guineas for a night's work. He wanted my opinion about a hydraulic stamping machine that jumped gear. He gave me his card, 'Colonel Lysander Stark.' The machine was at Eyford, in Berkshire, near Reading. We took the last train from Paddington, arriving about 11:15 last evening."

Hatherly described the hydraulic press: "It was like a room. The ceiling of the chamber was the end of the descending piston and it came down with the force of many tons upon a metal floor." The press sounded more diabolical than practical.

Holmes deduced that it had something to do with coinage. "They are coiners on a large scale and have used the machine to form the amalgam which has taken the place of silver," said the detective.

"We have known for some time that a clever gang was at work," interjected Inspector Bradstreet of Scotland Yard. He had joined the group on Holmes' summons. "They have been turning out half-crowns by the thousand."

The young engineer then described

the events of the previous night.
Suspecting an illicit purpose for the
press, he tried to leave but was
detained by Col. Stark. During his
escape, Hatherly lost a thumb, but
made his way back to London—to Dr.
Watson's, then to Sherlock Holmes'.

After learning of the Hatherly case,
I contacted Mr. E.G.V. Newman,
managing director of the London-
based Bureau for the Suppression of
Counterfeit Coins. I mentioned Half-
crowns of 1889 and he replied, "A
very common counterfeit, I have seen
more of that year than any other."
Newman gave me a photograph of one
particularly deceptive specimen.

And some say that Sherlock Holmes
lived only in the mind of Dr. Arthur
Conan Doyle!

**A young Victoria graced the
half-crowns of 1889**

THE MAN WHO MADE GOLD FOR THE U.S. MINT!

Rascals have a way of capturing our
imaginations. There have been con
men, too, whose ingenuity earned
them grudging admiration. Such was
the case of Dr. S.H. Emmens of New
York City. For two years, the U.S.
Mint believed Emmens had succeeded
where Merlin and Midas failed—to
turn baser metals into gold!

Dr. Emmens was no run-of-the-mill
quack. He had published papers on
chemistry, electricity, and metallurgy.
He was a member of the U.S. Board of
Ordnance and had received a patent on
a high explosive he called "Emmen-
site," later adopted by the U.S. Army.
Emmens was a novelist and a poet,
and he firmly believed that all forms of
matter were ultimately one (or so he
said); thus silver could be turned into
gold. Emmens successfully explained
his intriguing discovery to the U.S.
Mint.

The good doctor convinced Treasury
officials that the silver in Mexican
pieces of eight contained certain
impurities and that by chemical
evolution some of the silver could be
transmuted into gold, or into a new
substance he called *argentaurum*, an
amalgam of gold and silver. By
mechanical treatment, Emmens said
he could separate the two metals. He
theorized that the silver could be
turned back into coinage and the
remaining gold would be profit.

Treasury officials were not alto-
gether trusting. While they bought Dr.
Emmens' *argentaurum gold*, they
assayed every purchase. Between
April and December, 1897, the mint
purchased 661.01 ounces. The fineness varied from .305 to .751 fine.
Emmens explained the variances by
pointing out that Mexican eight-reales
were struck at several different mints,

so the amount of "impurities" varied, affecting his ability to extract *argentaurum*. During the next year the Mint purchased more gold, some of it assaying as high as .997.

The Mint was silent on the fact that it was buying "artificial gold" and coining it into two-and-a-half-, five-, ten-, and twenty-dollar gold pieces. The secret remained theirs until the *New York Herald* headlined a story, "Man Makes Gold and Sells It To The United States Mint." The government thereupon owned up to its dealings with the modern-day alchemist.

More careful analysis of the *argentaurum gold* revealed its impurities to be similar to those found in old gold jewelry. Emmens was exposed as a fraud, but no one is yet sure of his real reasons. The gold sent to the Mint

The eight-reales of Mexico was the most common of all silver coins issued by the Republic and one of the world's most important trade coins.

was real enough; Emmens had to pay for it to sell it. He had no backers nor did anyone "invest" in his scheme. If any fraud was perpetrated, it was by our own government in believing that the gold they were buying was the work of a wizard in a laboratory and not that of Mother Nature.

DR. S.H. EMMENS—A SEQUEL

Before the "eminent" Doctor S.H. Emmens appeared on the scientific scene, writing articles for scholarly journals, producing special explosives for the United States Army, and introducing the U.S. Mint to *argentaurum gold* extracted from Mexican eight-reales coins, he had spent some time in Denver with a mint-related effort. Dr. Emmens, then known as Fernando Newman, promoted a "wonderful little machine" capable of manufacturing shiny, brilliant, uncirculated five-dollar pieces.

In 1888, Dr. Emmens was a transient resident of Denver's Hotel Windsor. Although he spoke abominable Spanish, many of his clients accepted his word that he was a direct descendant of Don de Dorsey Pedro Sanchez y Lopez, whoever that was. Emmens-Newman would find a mark, claim to have a friend in the United States marshall's office, and show his marvelous little machine that had been developed by his royal forbear. It was shaped like an alarm clock, with gears and cranks and dials. Emmens would insert a specially prepared compound of cheap base metal in one end. He would then turn cranks and keys, and through a secret process, new five-dollar gold pieces would spill out the other end. Emmens claimed his secret processed half-eagles were as good as the U.S. Mint's and cost only a fraction of the face value to make. The pieces should have looked good—

for they were genuine United States Mint products! For $2,000 cash, Dr. Emmens would supply sufficient base metal for one month's production.

From Denver, Emmens traveled west to San Francisco, finding buyers for his "little mint" along the way. The scam gave birth to the idea of "extracting" gold from silver eight-reales that he demonstrated for Mint officials a few years later.

Between these two scams, Emmens floated fake mining schemes and industrial ventures. While in Colorado he did a play on the name of one of the great gold producing mines—the Independence in Victor, Colorado, and formed "The Independence Extension." His choice of name worked beautifully for a while and when the sucker lists were worked over, he formed the Gold Syndicate. He offered a monthly dividend of one percent and a semi-annual bonus amounting to fifty-four percent per annum. Rubes waiting to part with their money could not resist. When that scam started to play out, Emmens went east. He was Dr. Emmens once again, claiming to have discovered the means to suspend the laws of gravitation. When the crowds thinned, he turned to extracting gold from silver coin.

To some, Dr. Stephen H. Emmens was a great scientist; to most though, he was a bunco artist without peer. His victims numbered in the hundreds and included officials of the United States Mint. His gold scam with the Mint it seems, was no more than a means of disposing of stolen gold jewelry.

Crude, with meaningless dates and legends, Billies and Charlies are considered as much folk art as numismatic novelties.

BILLY AND CHARLEY

William Smith and Charles Eaton were a couple of amiable rascals. The larceny in their hearts was directed more toward earning a few pence than dishonest endeavor. Billy Smith and Charley Eaton lived long before minimum wages or social welfare, when poverty was accepted and a few cents a day was all that some could expect to earn.

Billy and Charley were mudlarks, scavengers along the tidal flats that marked the shoreline of the Thames River. Their livelihood consisted of searching for scraps of metals, lumps of coal, anything salvageable, and selling it for the few pence they desperately needed. Uneducated, illiterate, Smith and Eaton mucked their way to minor fame in the mid-1840s. In a stretch of the imagination, they rank with the Earl of Sandwich, the Lords Chesterfield and Cardigan, and other Britons whose names have

become generic. *Billies* and *Charlies* are a particular kind of collectible, considered examples of folk art.

A single incident launched these two into an enterprise that would spark collector interests more than a century later. The chance finding of a genuine pilgrim's badge along the foreshore of the Thames near London's Shadwell district, started Smith's and Eaton's careers in forgery. The pilgrim's badge brought only a few shillings from the Bristol Museum, but that was more than the two had earned at any one time in their lives.

News of their discovery brought collectors to watch the mudlarks' labors, but offers to purchase any new finds went unfulfilled, nor did they find items of "antiquity". Smith and Eaton considered their fleeting fame and their chance to earn a few bob. If they could find no more antiques, why not make a few?

Billy and Charley could not read or write, but they did not lack ingenuity. Obtaining a horse brass, a harness medallion, they traced the outline on a flat piece of chalk. For a central figure, they drew the head of a man, capped him with a helmet, and scribbled a meaningless legend around. Wording, they knew, was not as important as date. With a little advice, they chose a date in the eleventh century—the older the better, they decided. Their product was cast in *cock metal*, a low grade pewter, but it looked too new. Dipping it in an acid solution solved the problem. Salting their piece in the mudflats, Billy and Charley promptly redis-covered it. An eager buyer snapped it up and Smith and Eaton were in business.

Total production over the next few years numbered in the hundreds. The dates of their creations ranged from the early eleventh through the six-teenth centuries. Smith and Eaton's designs were a hodgepodge of ancient and medieval costumes and their product line also included small metal vases and figurines.

In 1857, when excavations began along the tidal flats to sink foundation pillars for Shadwell Docks, hundreds of these forgeries were found. Today they are collected as intriguing pieces of folk art in numismatic form. The gullible extended past the collectors of the period. Several years ago, a pair of *Billies* and *Charlies* toured the United States as part of a Byzantine collection!

MRS. BUTTERWORTH'S PATTERNS

When Ebenezer Butterick patented his technique for printing and cutting paper dressmaking patterns in 1846, the 21-year old shirtmaker believed he had invented a new process. Butterick would have been distressed to learn that his method had been used at least 131 years earlier by a woman with a similar name. Mary Peck Butterworth originally developed the technique— for making money! Mrs. Butterworth's method of reproducing currency was exact enough to cause the recall of the colonial Rhode Island five-pound note of July 5, 1715.

The lady counterfeiter of Massachu-setts Bay Colony was a housewife, the mother of seven children and made money-making part of her household chores. While Mrs. Butterworth's process required patience and a steady hand, she needed none of the skills of a plate maker, printer or engraver. Her system was simple: she took a dampened piece of starched muslin cloth, placed it over a genuine bill, pressed lightly with a hot iron, and a negative impression of the note would transfer onto the cloth. This "pattern" would be placed on a blank piece of paper and *ala* Butterick, ironed onto the surface. With a fine pen, Mrs. Butterworth would trace over the impression of the note-to-be, enhancing the design and the lettering. The transfer pattern was always burned, destroying any possible incriminating evidence.

Mary Peck Butterworth's cottage industry grew--her line soon included Connecticut notes of five-pound value; Massachusetts Bay bills of forty shillings, three pounds and five pounds; Rhode Island notes of ten shillings, three pounds-twenty shillings, and five pounds. To meet the growing demand, she added several family members to the clandestine payroll. Her brother, Israel Peck, joined her as a pen maker and tracer. Brothers Nicholas and Stephen were recruited, along with Nicholas' wife, Hannah who became as adept as Mrs. Butterworth in lettering. The products were sold at half face by two of Mr. Butterworth's hired hands, along with the town's deputy sheriff.

The quantity of unofficial currency caused great concern among the authorities. Suspicion fell upon the innocent court judge, Daniel Smith, and his home was searched for the engraving plates. The demise of the Butterworth enterprise began with the apprehension of one of the hired hands while passing a spurious bill. His capture led to the arrest of the other hired hand and the latter confessed on the promise of leniency.

The double arrests led to a raid on Mrs. Butterworth's kitchen, but authorities were unable to find the incriminating currency plates needed to sustain a conviction. All were released. Mrs. Butterworth turned to more conventional domestic pursuits and lived to be 89. Perhaps it was her

story, documented in the historical archives of the Massachusetts township of Rehoboth, that prompted Ebenezer Butterick to move the process of pattern transfer from the kitchen to the sewing room.

A counterfeited Rhode Island note, dated July 5, 1715. All were recalled in 1727 because of the counterfeiting.

DR. SAMUEL HIGLEY WAS AN UNUSUAL MAN!

Samuel Higley was an unusual man. Although he had his medical degree from Yale, he was a practicing blacksmith. He invested in business enterprises, including one to make money—his own!

Higley hung his shingles in Granby, a small town north of Hartford, Connecticut. In 1728, he speculated in land within the shadows of Peak Mountain. Having dabbled in metallurgy, Higley suspected the area had great mining potential. Within a year he was exporting copper to England.

The average man would have been satisfied with any one of Higley's three occupations--successful mine owner and operator, experienced blacksmith, busy physician and general practitioner. But Dr. Samuel Higley was no ordinary man. He knew his ore was going to England to be used in copper coinage of the day. Why not, he reasoned, make his own money right in Granby? Using his blacksmith equipment and ore from his own mine, Higley hammered out his first coins. On them he placed a value of three pence, but local merchants challenged him. His coins were the size of the circulating half-pence and he claimed a value of six times as

great. He responded by changing the denomination to: "Value Me As You Please," adding, "I am good copper."

The Connecticut doctor produced many coin designs and varieties. On one he depicted an axe and placed around it the words, "I cut my way through," hopefully not referring to his medical practice! The most unique of all his coins bore the picture of a wheel. Quite profoundly he added the statement, "The wheele goes round." Only a single specimen of this coin is known to have survived the more than 200 years since it was first struck. A 1737 example from the collection of Johns Hopkins University was sold in 1980 for a mere $75,000!

It is not known how many coins Dr. Higley made. No more than a dozen examples of each of his other designs have survived, although they are known to have circulated widely around the Granby area for many years. Ironically, the quality of the copper contributed to their disappearance from circulation. The words, "I am good copper," proved very true. Higley's coins were highly valued and sought after, but not by his neighbors who had accepted them in change. Contemporary goldsmiths found the high grade of copper a desirable alloy for their gold, which accounts for the scarcity of Higley's coins today.

Value Me As You Please, and *I Cut My Way Through* were Dr. Higley's responses to criticism of the values he placed on his homemade money.

WHEN NICKELS TURNED TO GOLD!

In the days of King Arthur's Round Table, charlatans and wizards supposedly spent their lives chanting incantations and concocting secret formulae for changing base metal into gold. Centuries later, in 1883, some succeeded—with the help of the United States government.

Early in the year a newly designed five-cent piece—the Liberty head nickel—was introduced. Classic in design, the engravers took artistic license and intentionally omitted the word "five cents" from the coin. Since the coin was approximately the same size as the five-dollar gold piece, it was only a matter of weeks before modern-day charlatans began gold washing or plating the new nickels and upvaluing them in trade. Some even made a tooling device to reed the edges.

The omission of the work "cents" was not in error as many numismatic researchers like to claim. It was intentional. In 1881, at the request of Colonel A.L. Snowden, director of the Mint, chief engraver Charles E.

Barber prepared designs for a nickel cent, a nickel three-cent coin, and a nickel five-cent piece. Here was an omnibus design in classic simplicity for the reverse—a Roman numeral within a wreath to designate the denomination. All obverses were Liberty heads, similar to the one designed for the new five-cent coin.

The idea of not placing the actual denomination on the coin was not new. The first half-dimes, dimes and quarters issued by the U.S. Mint omitted any reference to face value. The first half-dollars carried the value around the edges only.

In the 1883 wave of immigration to the U.S. were people who did not understand the language and were readily tricked and cheated; and there were also those ready to take advantage of the situation. The practice of gold washing or plating the new five-cent piece became so widespread that the Mint was forced by midyear to add the words "five cents" to the 1883 nickel.

The newcomer to America was not the only one fooled; the wily collector fared little better. Over five million five-cent pieces without the denomina-

The words "five cents" were intentionally omitted from the first issues of the Liberty head nickel, giving rise to

the procedure of gold plating the coins and passing them for five-dollar gold pieces.

tion were coined before the Mint started production of those with the value on the reverse. The Mint then struck three times as many as were made during the next three years combined. Everyone saved the coins with the "mistake"—the one without the words "five cents." So many were stashed that until a few years ago, one could buy a specimen in extra fine condition for less than a dollar. Everyone saved the scarcer issue and spent the more common one, causing it to wear and disappear from circulation.

The Liberty head nickel of 1883, without the words "five cents," gave the English language the expression "to *josh* someone." Joshua Tatum, a deaf mute, was one of the first to turn nickel into gold by washing. His con was to make a five-cent purchase and place one of his golden nickels on the counter. If the merchant gave him $4.95 in change, and most did, who was defrauding whom? A popular retort on getting one's hand caught in the cookie jar was, "But, I was only *joshing*."

No kidding!

HITLER DIARIES NOT THE ONLY FAKES

When the purported diaries of Adolf Hitler were exposed during the summer of 1983 as "blatant, grotesque and superficial" forgeries, the news came as no surprise to numismatic scholars. The hobby has long been subjected to equally blatant counterfeit coins of Hitler.

Nazi Germany issued no general circulation coins bearing the portrait of Adolf Hitler, although it is believed that the Berlin Mint experimented with pattern designs bearing the Fuehrer's portrait in 1942. One

exceedingly rare five-mark pattern has been catalogued and is listed in the Standard Catalog of Modern World Coins. A second pattern, also attributed to the Berlin Mint, has been reported but not confirmed. These two pieces are the only known Hitler coins.

A 1933 100-reichsmark gold pattern has a history similar to the diaries. Supposedly presented personally by Hitler to the father of a German collector, the "coin" has as many errors as the alleged diaries.

The "coin" was made in .333 fine gold; coin gold is .900 fine. Surely a tribute to the German leader would not have been issued in a debased metal! Just as the monograms appeared incorrectly on the covers of the diaries, the German word for pattern, *probe*, is misspelled with a *d* instead of a *b* on the "coin."

Another fantasy, well struck but clumsily designed, is sometimes offered as a "pattern" to Hitler buffs and collectors. Hitler is identified in English rather than German. *Adolph* is used instead of *Adolf*! A further discrepancy is the listing of the terminal dates—1889 for Hitler's birth, 1945 for his death. Immediate postwar Germany had no time or inclination to honor the man who brought shame and destruction on the country.

The most cleverly produced forgery of a Hitler coin may have come from Italy. Dated 1938, the piece carries a value of one reichsmark and the German eagle with swastika is cleverly copied from the German two-reichsmark, perhaps to imply that this coin is the companion piece to the Hindenberg issue of 1936.

Although Nazi Germany issued no coins with Hitler's portrait, his rule was noted on both general circulation and commemorative issues. In 1936, existing designs of regular issue coins—the one-, two-, five- and ten-reichspfennigs—were modified to include a swastika on the reverse. In 1938 the fifty-reichspfennig was similarly changed. In 1934, commemorative two- and five-reichsmark coins appeared, depicting the Potsdam Garrison Church in recognition of the first anniversary of Nazi rule. It was at the Garrison Church in 1933 that Hitler offered the symbolic handshake to Hindenberg to symbolize the melding of Germany's illustrious past with its hopes for an even greater future. In 1936, swastikas were added to the Hindenberg commemoratives of the previous years.

There are legitimate German issues with Hitler's portrait, but these are tokens, not regular issue coins. The Law of 1925 forbade the collecting of money at political rallies. Hitler, in his rise to power, needed funds badly. To circumvent the law, special souvenirs were issued and sold at political gatherings. Included were postcards and specially made "donation tokens," bearing Hitler's portrait.

Purported patterns offered as coins

BUTCH CASSIDY—AND NATIONAL BANK NOTES

During Butch Cassidy's Hole-in-the-Wall Gang heyday, the principal United States currency was National Bank Notes, issued from 1863 to 1935. The banks involved were organized under the National Currency Act and were required to deposit with the treasurer of the United States, a specified amount in U.S. bonds. When the deposit was made, the comptroller of the currency would issue authorization for the bank to do business. The bank could then issue notes equal to ninety percent of the bonds it had on deposit. Design of the notes was up to the Treasury and space was left on the National Bank Notes to overprint the bank's charter number. The National Currency Act of 1863 required that each note be signed by the cashier and the bank's president or vice president—hand signed, rubber stamped, or printed. The signatures always appeared at the bottom of the face of the note, the cashier signing on the left and the president or vice president on the right. The notes were shipped to the banks without the signatures.

On June 2, 1899, there was an armed robbery of a Union Pacific train at Wilcox, Wyoming. Some $3,400 of unsigned currency belonging to the First National Bank of Portland, Oregon, was taken. Although they were accused of the heist, there was no proof that Robert Leroy Parker (Butch Cassidy) or Harry Longabaugh (the Sundance Kid) were involved. Cassidy was reportedly working as a ranch hand in New Mexico at the time.

However their innocence is not so easily established in another train robbery—a Great Northern Railway train near Wagner, Montana, on July 3, 1901. This time $40,000 in unsigned notes of the National Bank of Helena, Montana, was taken. Cassidy was identified as one of the bandits. Hole-in-the-Wall cohorts—the Sundance Kid and Camilla "Deaf Charley" Hanks, were named with Butch as the culprits. Several months later, Ben "Tall Texan" Kilpatrick was arrested and charged with the armed robbery. Seven thousand of the $40,000 of unsigned notes was found in his possession. Kilpatrick's arrest led to the apprehension of Harry Logan, better known as Kid Curry. Logan had an additional $10,000 of the unsigned notes in his possession. The finger of guilt pointed correctly to the third man, Deaf Charley, but he was never apprehended for this robbery, nor was $23,000 in unsigned National Bank of Montana notes ever recovered.

The National Bank of Montana had been chartered only six months when the train robbery occurred. The unsigned notes had been printed four up—three ten-dollar and one twenty-dollar—by the Bureau of Engraving and Printing. Until the bank closed and consolidated with the First National Bank & Trust Company of Helena on May 23, 1931, a total of 164,036 large sized notes totaling $2,050,450 had been issued; only $22,640 remained outstanding on closing day. Assuming some notes were lost or destroyed, others were in collectors' hands, is it safe to assume that Butch Cassidy and the Sundance Kid took other aliases and turned to forgery, signing the names of the cashier and president? For collectors, the notes of the First National Bank of Montana are worth checking.

An unsigned note of the National Bank of Montana at Helena

THE CASE OF THE AGED INVENTOR

By 1911, *Scientific American* was already in its sixty-seventh year of publication. Billed as the "weekly journal of practical information," the inventors' magazine carried a column called "The Laboratory." One of the writers was Alfred J. Jarman. The column featured suggestions for "home experiment." Jarman took his editorial assignment too literally.

Alfred Jarman lived in inventors' simplicity in a small furnished room in Newark. As he neared retirement age, Jarman hinted to fellow employees at the journal that he had a new invention, an inexpensive gadget that could put him "on easy street."

On December 9, 1911, the old inventor was arrested as a result of complaints by neighborhood shopkeepers. They all knew and liked him, but they noticed that whenever he made a purchase, one or two cast dimes would turn up in their cash drawers.

Secret Service agent John J. Henry had been assigned to the case of the bad dimes. For a while Henry shadowed Jarman, checking registers and cash boxes after every purchase. His suspicions confirmed, Henry obtained a warrant to search Jarman's room. Here he found a melting pot, a ladle, some white metal and two counterfeit dimes.

Jarman had been modest in his quest to be on "easy street." He made only a few coins at a time, just enough to supplement daily cash needs. None the less, Alfred Jarman held no patent on the manufacture of coins and was arraigned before a United States commissioner on the charge of counterfeiting dimes.

WAS THE PATRON SAINT OF COIN COLLECTORS COUNTERFEIT?

The name St. Eligius is seldom invoked today; few have ever heard of the seventh century cleric. But at one time he was a most popular saint. In his earthly days, Eligius was a bishop, a counselor to royalty, a missionary. He was also a craftsman, master of the royal mints at Paris, Marseilles, and Limoges; the designer of many coins, leading to his selection as the guardian saint of goldsmiths, silversmiths, jewelers, blacksmiths—patron to mintmasters and coin collectors.

The best known depiction of St. Eligius is a fifteenth century painting by Petrus Christus. Entitled *Saint Eligius*, it shows the venerable Saint as a goldsmith, weighing out gold for wedding bands while a young couple watches. But a modern day question

Saint Eligius as a goldsmith offers a realistic look at a fifteenth century jeweler's shop

18

arises, 'Did Christus intend this painting to honor the saint, or are the saintly markings a latter-day adaptation?' Is the common interpretation that Christus' work honors a saintly mintmaster—counterfeit?

Petrus Christus was a master of the Flemish school after the death of Jan van Eyck in 1440. His few extant works can be found in great museums, including *Saint Eligius as a Goldsmith* in the Lehman Collection at the Metropolitan Museum of Art in New York. However, the painting bears many titles and interpretations. It is also known as *The Legends of Saints Eligius and Godeberta*, and *St. Eligius and the Lovers*. There are scholars who believe that Christus worked at a time when wordly preoccupations had to be disguised and that Christus painted a goldsmith's shop under the pretense of glorifying St. Eligius. Some modern day art historians hold that Eligius' halo has a latter-day touch of gold added to give credence to the saintly rationale.

Eligius' introduction to coins came at an early age. The son of Roman-Gallic parents, Eligius was born at Chaptel, Gaul, in 588. His father was a metalsmith and apprenticed his young son to the master of the mint at Limoges. Following his apprenticeship, Eligius worked under the royal treasurer, and became master of the mint at Paris for King Clotaire I.

When the king wanted a new throne, Eligius' superiors were hesitant to make one, for they feared the king's disposition when he was disappointed. They assigned the task to Eligius. It was customary for the craftsman to keep surplus material after the completion of a project, and Eligius made not one but two thrones, the second more handsome than the first, decorating the second with the surplus gold. The king was so pleased

A tremissis of Dagobert I, 629-639, struck by Eligius as master of the Paris mint

that Eligius was amply rewarded. He used his reward money to ransom slaves, and the land presented to him to found several churches, monasteries and convents.

Eligius collected Roman and Greek coins, not as a numismatist, but to study them for design and manufacture. Eligius reportedly melted down his fine collection of ancient gold and silver coins for their precious metal, to make reliquaries for saints—not the act of a coin collector, but a good story of sacrifice to enhance the saintly image of the man.

Eligius coins are extremely rare and valuable today. One specimen, a tremissis of Dagobert I, son of Clotaire, struck at the Paris mint, brought $15,500 at the Numismatic Fine Arts sale of the Garrett Collection in October 1984.

The Godeberta attribution to Christus' painting is more difficult. There are those who interpret the scene as a visit to Eligius by Godeberta and her fiance to purchase their rings. Eligius instead slips his bishop's ring on Godeberta's finger, thus marrying her to Christ and the church.

Eligius, the patron saint of mintmasters and coin collectors, is a good example of a genuine character of antiquity. Counterfeit—definitely not; a little altered—maybe!

RENAISSANCE HOUSE

PUBLISHERS

541 Oak Street • P.O. Box 177

Frederick, CO 80530

GOIN' STRAIGHT TO THE SOURCE
Stories From the Mints

No specimen of an uncirculated ten-dollar Mormon gold piece is known to exist. Yet, out in the desert near Salt

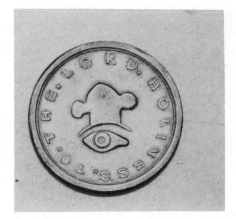

Lake City may be a cache of these coins. Value would be in excess of $25 million!

THE GHOSTS OF BULLOCK'S MONEY MILL

Room 509 is in the new section of Salt Lake City's Hotel Utah. The street traffic has long since ceased. You are sure other guests are asleep, you hear muffled sounds penetrating the four walls of your room. You're convinced you hear the thump of a blanking press, the meshing of gears of a rolling mill. You can sense the vibration of machinery and ever so lightly, feel the heat of a forced fire under a crucible of molten metal. For here, on this site, under this very room, 135 years earlier, was the Mormon Mint, then called "Bullock's Money Mill." It had been in operation since December 1848.

Salt Lake City was a route stop along the Overland Trail to California. Prospectors headed for the gold fields paused here to refresh and resupply, but did little business with Mormon merchants. The church people dealt primarily in barter or in scrip. Reportedly these passersby would not buy or sell anything except gold dust or coined money. Brigham Young, recognizing the importance of the transient trade, named Thomas Bullock and John Kay to study the feasibility of a Mormon coinage. Supporting Young's theory, Bullock and Kay secured the necessary equipment and ultimately produced a series of gold coins ranging from $2.50 to $20 in denomination. The twenty-dollar gold piece was the forerunner of the U.S. Mint's double-eagle, preceding the government issue by a year. Production at Bullock's extended from December 1848 until February 1862, when the need for private issue gold ceased.

No records have ever existed showing the actual number of coins produced. Accurate record keeping was unimportant to commerce. John Kay, the mint's bookkeeper, often overlooked daily entries and some-

THE MINT IN 1855

1. First store in Utah, where Hotel Utah now stands
2. Tithing Office
3. Brigham Young's stables
4. Mint where gold coins were made
5. Deseret News building
6. Brigham Young's first home
8. Bee Hive House
9. City Wall

times entered only the total number of coins struck—with no mention of denomination!

Coinage dates on Mormon coins were not changed on an annual basis. Coins struck from 1848 on were dated 1849. The only exceptions were the five-dollar gold pieces. Design changes in 1850 and 1860 did incorporate date changes on these coins.

The lackadaisical air around the mint extended to security: the facility was unguarded at night. There were neither bars on the windows nor a vault within the building, and the inevitable happened one night in 1850.

Gold attracted more than its share of ne'er-do-wells, including the Baldwin brothers, Dave and Reg. En route to the gold fields of California, the two stopped in Great Salt Lake City and visited the mint. They visually cased the building, and, that same night, made off with the day's production— 250 gold pieces conveniently left on Bullock's workbench. When morning brought discovery, a Mormon posse gave chase, south along the trail from Salt Lake City. But the Baldwins had first headed west, off the traveled path, and apparently escaped.

Years later, the next chapter emerged. A scouting party crossing the inhospitable Sevier Desert, 150 miles southwest of Salt Lake City, found the remains of two men later identified as the Baldwins. Bones of their horses and pack animals eventually were found half-buried along the desert sands. There was no trace of the Mormon gold coins. They may have fallen from the pack on one of the animals as it staggered across the desert in search of water. But very likely, in the desert southwest of Salt Lake City, is a string of 250 uncirculated Mormon gold coins. If they were ten-dollar gold pieces, they are worth up to $100,000 each. Not one has ever been recorded in uncirculated condition. Even if they were the more common five-dollar gold pieces, the total value catalogs at more than $2.5 million.

It may have been the restless spirits of the Baldwin brothers disturbing the atmosphere in room 509, trying to tell where their bounty lies.

THE FIRST DENVER MINT ROBBERY

We all play an occasional role in history, and James D. Clarke's part was first robber of the Denver Mint. Clarke was paymaster at the Treasury facility and on February 13, 1864, decided he deserved a small bonus. He helped himself to $36,815.05.

James Clarke should not be confused with Austin Clark or his brother Milton, founders of Clark, Gruber and Company, predecessors to the United States Mint at Denver. Their company had been sold to the U.S. Government the previous April for $25,000. Clark, Gruber and Company had been formed in Leavenworth, Kansas, in 1858. Noticing the amount of gold reaching them from the Pikes Peak region, the group decided there was a need for a bank and a mint in the Denver area. The minter-to-be correctly assumed that the miners and business people of Denver would welcome such an enterprise. The first coins of the Clark, Gruber mint appeared in the summer of 1860. The legality of a private mint was questioned in the territorial legislature, so in 1863 the minting facilities were sold to the U.S. Government. The bank remained in private hands, evolving into the First National Bank of Denver.

James D. Clarke was twenty-one years old when he emigrated from

Pennsylvania in 1863. Initially employed as a bookkeeper for the *Rocky Mountain News* and well-liked, young Clarke sought and received the recommendations of H.P. Bennett, Colorado's territorial delegate to Congress, and Amos Steck, mayor of Denver. With such support, Clarke received his appointment as pay clerk for the Mint on December 30, 1863. Six weeks later he was a wanted man.

Four days after the discovery of the theft, George W. Lane, superintendent of the branch Mint at Denver, penned a letter to Salmon P. Chase, Secretary of the Treasury in Washington:

Denver City, Feby 19th, 1864

"Sir: On Monday morning 15th Inst about 10 o'clock it was discovered that the Assistant Treasurer's Office and the U.S. Br Mint Denver had been robbed of about thirty-seven thousand dollars.

"Suspicion at once rested on James D. Clarke the pay clerk who was not at his post and who we have since found absconded on horseback on the Saturday night previous. The exact loss is ascertained to be thirty-six thousand eight hundred and seventeen 05/00 dollars.

"We have found the route taken by Clarke and his apprehension is I think only a question of time and we are hourly expecting to hear of the same. From the fact that our time and attention has been fully absorbed by our efforts to apprehend the culprit I trust you will pardon any seeming delay in imparting this information, further particulars will be given soon."

Yours with respect
Geo. W. Lane, Supt.
U.S. Br. Mint

Fortunately for the authorities, Clarke was better with figures than he was with horses. Clarke's loot from the Mint's safe included a bag of one-dollar gold pieces, a gold bar, and bundles of treasury notes. With some of the paper, he immediately set out to buy a horse, but neither he nor the horse had a good eye for a bargain—the nag was blind in one eye. Clarke also purchased a saddle, saddle bags, spurs, two pistols and a revolver. If he were to be chased, Clarke reasoned, he would be prepared.

As he headed southeast toward the Kansas border, the gold ingot, weighing about ten pounds, proved cumbersome, and he pitched it along the route. Before the week was over, Clarke had been apprehended—without his horse. The nag had turned its one good eye toward Denver and headed home without him.

While the townsfolk laughed at the greenhorn's futile attempt to escape via horseback, they were also somewhat sympathetic. The Denver Mint was not popular with many. When Clark, Gruber and Company sold their operation to the Government, everyone expected coin making would be continued, but Washington had different ideas. Although the Denver facility continued to be called a "mint," it operated as an assay office, handling the purchase and refining of gold. But, no coins were made and Denverites felt cheated.

Weeks after Clarke's capture, he walked out of jail and back to this old neighborhood. Most of the money had been recovered, except Clarke's expenses for the horse and equipment and one gold bar! No real effort was made to find him; he lunched with friends, visited others, and spent his nights on a cot under the stage of the Denver Theatre. After ten days of freedom, Clarke gave thought to discretion and headed north to work as a stock tender on a ranch near LaPorte. He was soon recognized by a deputy marshall who returned him to Denver. James D. Clarke stood trial and was convicted. His sentence: Leave Colorado Territory!

A POSTSCRIPT

When authorities apprehended James D. Clarke, they recovered most of the loot. The gold bar was eventually recovered too, but not in mint condition. The gold bar provides an interesting postscript to the story of The First Denver Mint Robbery.

When Clarke hurriedly quit Denver carrying the contents of the safe from the assistant treasurer's office at the Denver Mint, much of the currency was sewn into one of his saddle bags. The bag of one-dollar gold pieces fit neatly into the other bag, but the ten-pound gold bar presented a problem, so he pitched it. No attempt was made to hide it, nor was thought given to returning some day to recover it.

Fate brought two prospectors across Clarke's path the day after his escape. The young men had come to Denver to prospect for gold. They knew it came in dust, in flakes and in nuggets; that you either panned or dug for it. Never did they dream that gold came in brick form, already refined! Dumbfounded when they spotted a gold brick along their path, the pair became suspicious when they noticed that their gold bar carried the stamp of the U.S. Treasury. Both weight and fineness were also stamped into the brick. They were not so foolhardy, though, as to leave the bar where they found it, not to tell anyone else of their discovery.

Both were honest men, at least with each other. Returning to their lodgings, they carefully measured the bar and sawed it in half. They even saved their filings for their dust pokes. Neither was a numismatist, for they took hammers and pounded the mint markings into oblivion. With the markings illegible, one took his half not to a bank in Denver, but thirty miles west to the Kountze Brothers bank in Central City. The bank clerk knew gold was seldom found in such form and notified the authorities. The young prospector was arrested and he, in turn, implicated his friend who still had the other half.

Newspaper files do not indicate the sentence issued these two young entrepreneurs, but if they even had their hands slapped, they were punished more severely than the original perpetrator of the first Denver Mint robbery.

THE MAN WITH THE GOLDEN LEG

"Bitterness," said Harry Emerson Fosdick, "blinds life." The famed pastor of the Riverside Baptist Church in New York possibly had Orville Harrington in mind, for here was a bitter man. Harrington's resentment had its roots in a boyhood hunting accident that severely damaged his sciatic nerve and cost him his right leg through a series of amputations, each one promising to be the last, each promising relief from his severe pain.

Despite his handicap, Harrington pursued his childhood dream of becoming a mining engineer. He graduated from the Colorado School of Mines in 1898, but was only able to find work at the United States Mint at Denver. In 1909, he quit the Mint to accept a position that offered prestige

A contemporary newspaper sketch shows how Orville Harrington took gold from the Denver Mint:

1. Inserts a gold bar in his hollow leg
2. From the refinery. walks down the mint steps
3. Checks with the guard
4. Crosses the street to take a trolley home

and travel: Harrington was to be the superintendent of a copper mining project in Cuba. But within a short time, his handicap cost him his job.

By 1919, Harrington was back at the Mint in Denver, earning the munificent sum of four dollars per day, as the second shift supervisor in the mint's refinery—four dollars a day for a man with a college degree and the potential to be one of the great mining engineers of the day! Harrington believed he was worth much more to the Mint, and if they would not pay him what he was worth, he would pay himself—at the Mint's expense.

At the close of second shift on September 2, 1919, Harrington accepted the first payment "due" him in the form of a twelve-pound gold bar. Hiding it was simple—his artificial leg was hollow. The bonus payment was worth $1,400. As the mood moved him, Harrington advanced himself payments in the form of little gold bars, seven inches long, three and one-half inches wide and one inch thick. It was not until February 1920, that Harrington believed he had been justly compensated. By then the Mint was $81,400 short on its gold supply and Mint officials were aware of a shortage. Their only uncertainty—who was taking it.

Gold in the form of coin was one thing, but it was not easily negotiable in the form of Government bars. Harrington had, however, given thought to converting the bars to cash. He would simply sell it back to the Mint! Orville Harrington searched the real estate records for the mining towns of Cripple Creek and Victor, Colorado. He planned to lease a played out mine, melt his bars, add a few impurities, and sell it back to the Mint as new gold. Harrington would show his supervisors that his degree from the Colorado School of Mines was more meaningful than they realized and that having a handicap would not deter him.

When the superintendent of the Denver Mint, Thomas Annear, found that the mint's gold supply was dwindling faster than it should, he called in the Denver chief of the Secret Service, Rowland K. Goddard. All refinery workers were placed under surveillance and one after another were eliminated as suspects until three remained. A gold brick was planted, a stakeout set, and Orville Harrington took the bait.

Arrested, Harrington pleaded guilty and was sentenced to ten years at the Federal Penitentiary at Leavenworth, Kansas. After serving three and one-half years, the former Mint employee was paroled. He returned to Denver and worked for the city, again as a supervisor with bricks, but this time paving bricks laid by street crews. The irony may have been too much for Orville Harrington. He quit his job, deserted his family, and left the area, perhaps still in pursuit of his elusive dream.

THE GREAT DENVER MINT ROBBERY

The year was 1967. Jack Koch was executive director of the American Numismatic Association. I was the editor of *The Numismatist*. We had been invited to the Denver Mint for the swearing-in ceremony of Mrs. Marian Rossmiller, President Lyndon Johnson's choice to head the world's most efficient mint.

District Judge Neil Horan officiated at the ceremony and Miss Eva Adams, director of the Mint, observed. Protocol dictated that the more important guests be as close to the principals as possible. Jack and I were far back by the door, dressed in navy blue suits, white, narrow-collared Arrow shirts, and thin black ties. As the ceremony ended and the reception line formed, a little silver-haired lady winked as

she passed us and furtively whispered, "It's nice to see you Secret Service agents doing your job!" Moments later a uniformed guard tapped me on the shoulder and asked me to follow him. I pictured the headlines in *Numismatic News*, "Former Editor Charged With Impersonating Officer."

The guard led me to a spot near the West Colfax Avenue entrance, where an obsolete sentry box commanded a panoramic view of the main door. Pointing high on the marble facade, the guard said, "That's where one of the bullets hit during the Great Denver Mint Robbery of '22." I guess he wanted a fellow "officer" to know that there could be excitement and danger guarding the country's small change presses.

It was several years before I researched the Denver Mint Robbery. It had touches of Mack Sennett and the Keystone Cops, yet it was a tragic event—one guard and one of the robbers were killed. Ironically, the target was not a product of the Mint, but paper currency held there as a favor to the Denver Branch of the Federal Reserve Bank of Kansas City. Their own vaults were not as secure as those within the walled fortress of the Denver Mint.

The stage had been set much earlier for Denver's "Crime of the Century". The vault of the Federal Reserve branch bank at 16th and Lawrence Streets, was not adequate to hold large amounts of currency, so an agreement had been reached to have the Mint serve as a depository. Mint officials expressed concern and asked the Federal Reserve to use the rear doors behind heavy iron gates, out of sight of passersby, just as the Mint shipped its own coins. But the Feds preferred to park before the main entrance and carry bundles of cash down the front steps to a waiting truck. Security officers at the Federal Reserve Bank felt that robberies happened in darkened recesses, never in open view. Monday, December 18, 1922, proved them wrong. Evidently more than just disinterested passersby had watched and timed earlier transfers.

At 10:20 a.m. the Federal Reserve Bank's wire-meshed, open paneled, pick-up truck pulled up to the front of the Mint. Two hundred thousand dollars was waiting, assembled in ten packs, each weighing eight pounds, containing 4,000 crisp, new five-dollar Kansas City Federal Reserve Notes Series 1915. Two guards evenly divided the packs and carried them down the Mint steps, supervised by unarmed bank officer Joseph E. Olson. At that instant, a black 1922 Buick touring sedan pulled alongside the truck. Two men jumped out, joined by two "pedestrians." One yelled, "Hands up," and Denver's Crime of the Century was underway.

A contemporary post card shows the Denver Mint in 1922, year of the "Great Denver Mint Robbery"

One guard placed his half of the money in the back of the truck, dropped his gun and ran for cover. The other guard dropped his money in the street and dove under the truck. Charles Linton, a guard waiting inside the truck, whirled, tried to lock the truck doors and fired his service revolver. One of the holdup men fired at point blank range and the 65-year old Linton fell mortally wounded. Two of the guards inside the Mint entrance returned the fire, and a third sounded the alarm.

Soon there was greater pandemonium inside the Mint than on the street. A newspaper described the guard force as "mostly old, decrepit men." The senior guard panicked, pulled his service revolver, and raced through the corridors yelling unintelligible commands. The Federal Reserve officer, caught in the crossfire between the bandits and the Mint guards, reached the safety of the Mint only to be mistaken for one of the bandits. Fortunately they let him "surrender." Other guards rushed to the Mint windows and commenced firing. A picture was shot off the wall

1924. United States Mint and State Capitol, Denver, Colo.

in a cleaning establishment a block away. Windows were shot out of the hotel across the street. Two of the bandits were hit, one superficially, the other mortally.

A police car responding to the alarm was demolished before it could reach the scene, two blocks from the station. A cub reporter became so excited that he gave his story to the wrong newspaper. And the get-away car got away.

Denver in 1922 was an isolated community. Police set up road blocks to encircle the city, but the bandits stayed downtown. A week later, working on a tip, police found the body of Nicholas Trainor, frozen stiff, still sitting in the front seat of the stolen Buick. The others got away—at least for the time being.

Investigators traced the thieves to St. Paul, Minnesota. The stolen money was offered for sale at a discount—the serial numbers were known. Half the loot (one hundred thousand dollars) was later recovered, but no one was ever arrested, tried or convicted.

The bullet hole inside the Mint was the result of a mint employee's wild shot. The guard who pointed it out to me has long since retired. That's just as well; I wouldn't want to shatter a fellow "officer's" illusions.

This postscript to the story should interest collectors. When the Federal Reserve Bank reissued the stolen money, it not only eliminated any chance of tracing the stolen bills, but gave collectors a slim chance of having two bills, printed at different times, with the same serial numbers.

UNCLE SAM—BENEVOLENT FENCE!

New York streets were no safer in 1909 than they are today; apartments, tenements and flats no more secure. Thieves then, however, found a benevolent fence for their stolen goods in Uncle Sam. The New York Assay Office readily bought "scrap" jewelry and paid full bullion value for it—no questions asked.

In June 1909, chagrined officials noted that the United States Treasury was being made an "accomplice to burglars," and that a sizable quantity of suspect gold was being purchased for transformation into U.S. coin. Orders were issued to Superintendent Kingsbury Foster that the New York Assay Office should no longer buy scrap gold without a complete explanation of where it was produced. Treasury officials conceded that it was comparatively easy for industrious burglars to melt down gold watches, rings, and other articles to sell to the Government. During the prior fiscal year, 10,898 melts from gold deposits were made. Of this number, 995 (roughly ten percent) were articles of jewelry and "manufacturers' samples." Some were undoubtedly legitimate, but New York police officials suspected that many were not.

For a thirty day period, police and New York Assay Office personnel cooperated in trying to end Uncle Sam's role as a fence. An NYPD central office man was stationed at the assay office to examine gold brought in for melt. At first the officer simply took the names of those making suspect deposits. Some regular depositors, suspicious that they were being watched, stopped bringing in gold. Others simply battered the jewelry into unrecognizable lumps or melted it into crude lumps.

Shortly after the Fourth of July, without explanation, the New York police withdrew their man from the assay office. No arrests were made, but police believed that some of the "regular" thieves had been frightened off. In truth, they had simply changed their mode of operation. Gold stolen on the streets and in the homes of New York was directed to pawnbrokers in New Jersey, particularly Newark. Traveling dealers then made the rounds of the Jersey pawn shops. Stolen gold now followed a chain from thief to fence to dealer, then back to the New York Assay Office, before going to Philadelphia to be made into gold coin.

The New York police compiled a list of twenty-five suspected pawn dealers, but said the information was insufficient to obtain a conviction. They withdrew their man from the assay office and surveillance was abandoned, hoping the problem would go away. It did—a quarter-century later when the government stopped making gold coin.

THE MEN WHO CLOSED THE CARSON CITY MINT

To the collector, coins bearing the CC mintmark of Carson City, Nevada, have a special allure. While the coins of the branch mint are, generally, obtainable, there are some rarities including the 1870-CC double eagle and the 1873-CC no arrows twenty-five-cent piece. Production at the Carson City Mint was sporadic, and coinage finally ceased in 1893 when officials realized that some mint employees were producing as much for themselves as they were for the Government. Andrew Mason, Superintendent of the U.S. Assay Office in New York, was given the unenviable

task of investigating shortages occurring under the supervision of fellow superintendent, J.W. Adams, of the United States Mint at Carson City.

On February 13, 1895, a shortage of 3,000 ounces of gold was reported by Superintendent Adams to the Secretary of the Treasury. The latter requested Mason to investigate, and by March 15, Mason had journeyed across the U.S. by train to begin his task. He commenced with the thoroughness of Sherlock Holmes, his Dr. Watson being one A.L. Gallagher of the United States Secret Service. Gallagher pried outside the mint; Mason's sleuthing was within the walls of the Treasury facility.

At first it appeared that the gold might have been lost through careless processing. The mint had switched from a sulphuric acid process to part gold from silver, to one of nitric-sulphuric, but examination found the latter as efficient as the former. Then Superintendent Mason found an intriguing entry into the record books. Melt no. 64, dated November 7, 1892, had been recorded as a "silver purchase." The original entry noted that it assayed 482.5 thousandths gold and 500 thousandths silver. A reassay "corrected" the records to show only 19.5 thousandths gold—946 thousandths silver, a deficiency in the gold value of $20,417.93!

Paying closer attention to melt records, Mason found other reports had been "corrected." Soon the shortfall of gold reached $75,549.75, an astronomical figure for the 1890's. By a careful process of elimination, the finger of guilt finally pointed to John T. Jones, an assistant melter and refiner. His co-worker in the refining room was absolved of guilt when records reflected that the alterations were done during periods of his absence. The thefts had been occurring since 1891!

As the authorities were about to arrest Jones, Secret Service agent A.L. Gallagher threw in a ringer. He found that a former mint employee, James H. Heney, had taken more than $20,000 of processed gold to the Reno Reduction Works for remelting and assay. Were Heney and Jones confederates, or was security at the Mint so loose that two men were stealing gold simultaneously? Although that was never established, both were arrested and each stood trial separately.

Heney presented an unusual defense, calling in an expert witness to say that the Mint's processing procedures were so inefficient that the unaccountable shortage was created by gold vanishing down the sewers. His witness produced "samples" from the sewer to prove his point. The jury was unable to reach a verdict and a mistrial was ordered. The Government did more homework in preparing for the second trial and Heney was convicted and sentenced to eight years. For good measure, he was also fined $5,000.

John T. Jones' trial was not so imaginative, but he did create enough doubt among the jurors to accomplish a hung jury. He, too, faced a judge for the second time, and like Heney, Jones was found guilty. His sentence was identical—eight years and a $5,000 fine.

Between the two, Superintendent Mason calculated the Government's loss to be in excess of $100,000. During the investigations and trials of Heney and Jones in 1895, the Carson City Mint refinery ceased operations and business was limited to the receipt of gold deposits. No coins were ever produced again at Carson City and by 1899, the Secretary of the Treasury reduced its status to an assay office— thanks in part to the unauthorized operations of John T. Jones and James H. Heney—two men who labored to turn a Government mint into one of their own.

EARTHQUAKE!

Periodically the earth rumbles gently somewhere along California's San Andreas Fault. Reporters reach for their references and newspaper readers are treated to another lesson in the theory of platetronics. In preparing their stories, few reporters fail to make comparisons with the great San Francisco Earthquake of 1906.

For the serious numismatist there is a tangential kinship to the San Francisco quake. Few coin club regulars have not viewed the U.S. Mint's film, "The Granite Lady." The film was released in 1974 as part of the Old San Francisco Mint's centennial. Narrated by actress Mercedes McCambridge, the twenty-eight minute award winning film relates the life of the Old Mint, including its role in the Great Earthquake.

When the earth shook that Wednesday morning, April 18, 1906, the shift of the crustal plates along the San Andreas Fault was felt as far away as Cape Town, South Africa. San Francisco's great City Hall, which had taken twenty years to build, crumbled in twenty seconds. Fire, fed by ruptured gas lines and encouraged by broken water mains, proved more destructive than the movements of the earth. There were two tremors and several aftershocks, but the fires raged for four days, threatening to raze every remaining building. Before it was over the fire destroyed 520 city blocks, consuming 28,000 buildings including eighty churches and thirty schools.

The film plays heavily on the Mint's role during the immediate post-quake days. The building withstood the shocks and its contents were saved from the fire by the heroic efforts of Frank A. Leach, Mint Superintendent, and his staff. All other financial institutions and the subtreasury in the city were destroyed, so the Mint became the financial center of the city, dispersing funds and redeeming promissory notes of the "other" banks. The judicious use of early newsreel films and the re-enactment of the Mint's role lent authenticity to the production, but the film overlooked the fact that some survivors tried to help themselves to the cash inside the Mint.

As with most disasters, the best of man is tempered by the worst in others. There were heroes, but there were looters as well. The mayor of San Francisco, Eugene Schmitz, ordered that looters be shot on sight and soldiers patrolled the streets. Near the Mint, a man was shot and killed as he cut the fingers from the body of a dead woman to get to her rings. Several of the less scrupulous decided to avail themselves to the mountains of coin they envisioned lying inside the mint. Thirty-four men died in futile attempts to enrich themselves with Mint samples for supplies.

THE FANTASY THAT CAME TRUE—BRIEFLY!

I was in the office of Henry J. Holtzclaw, Director of the Bureau of Engraving and Printing, having just completed a tour of the fortress where all our paper money is printed. Director Holtzclaw looked at me with an "I-can't-believe-it" grin, then started to laugh. "James Landis just gave my name as a reference," he chuckled, then told me the whole story.

James Landis had been a ten-year employee of the BEP. Although in a menial job, Landis shattered a record of ninety years. He stole $160,000 of newly printed twenty-dollar bills and almost made it a perfect crime.

Landis was a checker-distributor, his sole responsibility being to assemble banded currency bundles and deliver them to a wrapping machine, then take the sealed bundles to a secured vault area. How tempting, to handle millions of dollars daily and to fantasize on what one could do with a bundle or two! Landis' fantasy began to evolve into plan.

Not only was it impossible to get anything out of the Bureau, it was equally difficult to get something in. To succeed, Landis had to do both. His plan was simple: he would substitute blank paper for genuine currency. Twenty-dollar bills were the largest denomination one could cash without raising attention, so Landis targeted two "bricks" of new twenties.

After currency notes have been printed, numbered, inspected, trimmed and cut, they are taken to a banding machine to be pressed into "bricks." Four thousand notes to a stack, they are bound under great pressure and steel banded. The notes are then taken to a wrapping machine, covered with heavy brown paper, a Treasury seal glued to one end and a label with serial numbers, date and initials of the wrapper on the other end. The packages are stored in Bureau vaults until needed by a Federal Reserve Bank for circulation.

Landis began to watch the trash piles, pack-ratting a broken seal here, a wooden block there, a large piece of wrapping paper or a steel band. He ferreted these out of the Bureau, storing them until he had everything he needed to make two counterfeit bundles. Just as the government periodically changes the silk fibers in the currency notes, other changes are made, too. The wrapping paper for the bundles was changed on Landis and it took him another two months before he could secure two pieces of adequate size.

On December 30, 1953, Landis was set. Back to the Bureau he brought his bands, wrappings, blocks of wood and foremost, an exact amount of blank white paper cut to size to substitute for the genuine currency. The switch was made. Since date and serial numbers are paramount checks for currency bricks, Landis still had to soak them off the genuine bundles and add them to his homemade ones, which took only a few apprehensive minutes in the men's room. All that remained was to remove the real money. Placing the bills in a brown grocery bag and adding a pair of dirty dungarees to the top, Landis checked out for the day, opening the bag and waving a dirty trouser leg to the guard. He was motioned on.

Fate intervened, however. On the first working day after New Year's, an order for currency took a clerk directly to the skid with the blank paper currency. Ordinarily it would have been months before that skid was touched and, by then, impossible to trace those who had come in contact with it. The bundles were to be transferred to another skid. The handler's experience told him immediately that something was wrong with two of the bricks. He called his supervisor, the bundles were opened, and the fraud discovered. All area employees were summoned but James Landis was not among them. He had called in sick, already enjoying his new wealth.

In just five days, one of them a holiday, Landis had disposed of $27,800 dollars. Some he had generously given to relatives and some he had invested in his own fantasies, one of his first purchases being a $150 cashmere coat.

After serving his sentence, Landis sought further government employment. After all, had he not shown imagination and initiative on the job? All one had to do was to ask Henry Holtzclaw, and to facilitate that for everyone, Landis gave the Director's name as a reference!

THE GREAT PRETENDERS

THE LAST EMPEROR OF THE UNITED STATES

Fantasy is an ideal escape for a mind broken by financial disaster. Joshua Abraham Norton fancied himself Emperor of the United States and the Protector of Mexico. With the assumed sovereignty due royalty he even issued his own currency, which was accepted at face by his "subjects."

English born, Norton came to San Francisco in 1849 from the Cape of Good Hope. While others used the city as their base for sojourns to the Mother Lode country, Norton sought his fortune in real estate. Within three years he was one of the wealthy men about town. Next he planned to corner the rice market but failed, and disappeared from the city for five years.

Early in the fall of 1859 he returned —but not as Joshua Norton. He was now Norton I, by a proclamation he issued:

> "At the preemptory request and desire of a large majority of the citizens of the United States, I, Joshua Norton, formerly of Algoa Bay, Cape of Good Hope, now for the past nine years and ten months of San Francisco, declare and proclaim myself Emperor of these United States. *Norton I.*"

For the next twenty years he was costumed in a blue uniform complete with military epaulets, dress sword and silk cockade hat. San Francisco, known for its hospitality then as now, accepted not only Norton I, but the money and bonds he issued to sustain himself. Newspapers gave wide coverage to his edicts and escapades. Bank cashiers had strict orders to accept his currency if presented in reasonable sums. His entourage consisted of two mongrel dogs,

Emperor Norton

Bummer and Lazarus. Together they dined not lavishly but at least generously at the free lunch bars of the city's saloons.

Norton became such a part of the city that the Board of Supervisors paid for new uniforms out of the city treasury. His castle was a Sacramento Street rooming house, the rent for which was a budgeted item of the local Masonic lodge. He held court in the California Street offices of Wells Fargo and Company, when few customers were around. When he died in 1880, 10,000 attended his services, local and state officials and dignitaries among them.

Today his notes are extremely rare. None is know in denominations larger than fifty cents, or four bits of the day. In banker's terms the currency might be described as promissory notes, for they proclaimed that

"The Imperial Government of Norton I promises to pay the holder thereof the sum of Fifty Cents in the year 1880 with interest at 5 per cent. per annum from date, the principal and interest to be convertible, at the option of the holder, at maturity, into 20 years, 5 per cent. bonds, or payable in gold coin."

The notes were then dated and signed by Norton, legal tender of his imperial reign and penned evidence of the benevolence of the citizens of San Francisco.

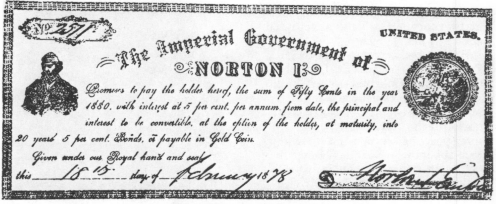

Fifty-cent note of Norton I

THE AMERICAN PRESIDENT OF NICARAGUA

Since Nicaragua became a nation in 1821, it has had relatively few years to enjoy its independence without civil strife or foreign intervention. History has made Nicaraguans leery of foreign intentions, including American. Commodore Cornelius Vanderbilt played political roulette to open a transisthmian route across the country in 1851 to shorten the journey to the California gold fields. An American canal across Nicaragua was fostered for decades. Americans have openly opposed presidencies from Zelaya to Ortega and supported rebel causes and oppressive dictatorships. In 1912, U.S. Marines landed and stayed until 1925. They returned the next year and remained until 1933, while Augusto Ceasar Sandino waged guerrilla warfare. A half century later, a revolutionary government calling itself *Sandinistas* in honor of Sandino, battle an American supported guerrilla movement. Few in the U.S. realize that an American adventurer, William Walker, ruled Nicaragua as its president from 1856 to 1857. Walker was the only native American to become head of a foreign nation.

William Walker was obsessed with power. Possibly realizing he could never be elected President of the United States, he tried to create his own republic. When this failed, Walker headed for Nicaragua and within a year of his arrival, ruled the country to the point of making his own money.

October 1853 found Walker and fewer than fifty men entering Mexico's Baja California. He proclaimed it an independent republic and named himself president. Supporting expansionism, Walker "annexed" the Mexican state of Sonora into his republic; but Mexico had had enough of the impertinent gringo and chased him back across the American border. Walker's Republic of Lower California lasted six months, and only in his mind.

Walker's 1855 invasion of Nicaragua was not the typical military incursion across a country's borders. The adventurer and his followers came on an invitation to join a rebel cause which promised land grants upon victory. Walker was soon commander-in-chief of the combined rebel forces. Six months later he was president of the country.

Walker's army, by now, was fair sized. He received support from some in the southern U.S. who foresaw America's Civil War and the need of a "friendly" ally. But Walker's men needed cash, not moral support, so he began seizing by decree, the lands of the "enemies of the republic." Walker recalled a few years later,

A fifty-dollar military payment scrip note signed by William Walker

"All property declared confiscated was to be sold soon after the rendition of judgment, and military scrip was to be received in payment at the sale of such property, thus giving those who had been in the military service of the state an opportunity to secure their pay out of the estates of the persons engaged in the war against them."

Since Walker's men were the only ones to possess this scrip, he liquidated his debt to them without cost to himself.

Walker printed his scrip in the plant of the *El Nicaraguense*, his own newspaper. The notes are exceedingly rare, only one or two examples surviving, as forgotten as the adventures of Walker himself. But Central Americans are reminded of Walker's escapades every time they view a monument in San Jose, the capital of Costa Rica. It allegorically portrays the five righteous republics of Central America—El Salvador, Guatemala, Honduras, Costa Rica AND Nicaragua —driving off the defeated American adventurer and former president of the Republic of Nicaragua, William Walker.

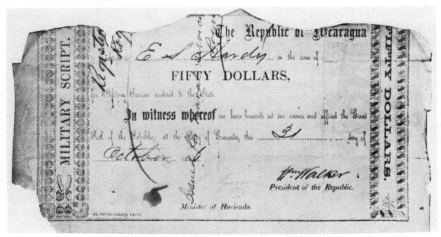

THE SAGA OF OUTER SPACE GOLD

Twenty years before Neil Armstrong set foot on the moon, an earthbound entrepreneur laid claim to the heavens, pressing his claim with the United Nations. Although ignored, James Thomas Mangan published books supporting his claim, sold titles, made appointments, issued passports, and produced an unusual series of coins and currency.

James Mangan surfaced in July 1947, when the United Press published a copyrighted interview in which Mangan stated that with a Government subsidy of $30 million, he could crack the secret of extrasensory perception. Many readers sensed a crack in the making. Eighteen months later, with no help coming from the U.S. Government, Mangan founded the Nation of Celestial Space, claiming all in the sky to be a sovereign territory. He named Evergreen Park, Illinois, the first capital, with his executive mansion at 3600 West 96th Street.

In February 1949, Mangan read that all agents of foreign governments need register with the state department. He attempted to comply as the "first representative" of Celestia. He formally notified all governments of the world of his claim to outer space. When the USSR launched its first sputniks, Mangan protested to the United Nations that his sovereignty had been violated. Mangan's most bizarre quest, though, was his attempted negotiations with Secretary of Agriculture Ezra Taft Benson, to load an experimental rocket with cactus seeds and fire it toward Venus in an attempt to start photosynthesis on that celestial body.

In 1958, First Representative James Thomas Mangan met with Second Secretary Sergei Bogomolov at the Soviet Embassy in Washington to argue over Soviet violations of Celestia's space. Like many earthbound nations, Celestia developed territorial ambitions of her own. On July 25, 1958, Mangan issued a proclamation declaring the Moon, Mars and her two moons, and the planet Venus, Protectorates of the Nation of Celestial Space. The United Nations secretariat was duly notified.

The next year Mangan promoted himself to premier and issued coins—gold celestons, little fourteen millimeter gold pieces about the size of a U.S. gold dollar. The obverse of these coins bore the portrait of Mangan's daughter, Ruth, whom he now referred to as "Princess." The word MAGNANIMITY appeared on the princess' headband, and magnanimity became Celestia's one-word slogan and "guiding philosophy." Eleven stars, each signifying a letter in the slogan, appeared around the obverse. The reverse of the coin read 1 GOLD CELESTON, NATION OF CELESTIAL SPACE, and a tiny mintmark signified the coin was made "in" space. Coins were issued for a number of years. By 1961, Mangan had advanced to prime minister and added silver coins and paper money to his nation's currency.

The few tangible reminders of the deceased premier's ambitious dream include some tiny coins found occasionally in dealer junk boxes as unidentified objects.

Gold celestons, reminders of a man's claim to space

THEY CALLED HIM THE MATCH KING

Ivar Kreuger didn't need to counterfeit; he made more real money illegally than most counterfeiters could ever print. Kreuger may have been the world's first billionaire, or at least he conned the world into believing so. Ivar Kreuger made his money playing with matches!

The self-proclaimed "Savior of Europe," the world knew Krueger as "The Match King." Too many found out too late that he was a master forger. The scale on which Kreuger operated defies exaggeration.

Kalmar, Sweden, at the time of Kreuger's birth in 1880, was the leading manufacturer of matches. The safety match had been developed there and one of Kreuger's successful goals was to control a monopoly on the making of matches. His International Match Company eventually controlled over seventy percent of the world production. But matches to Kreuger were mundane; flimflam held more excitement.

Trusting many transactions to memory (no bookkeeper would be *his* undoing) Kreuger borrowed money from one to loan to another, without intent of repaying the first, whole countries included. Starting with balances and working backwards, he faked financial reports and mortgaged company assets without informing lenders. Collateral for other loans were forged shares and securities. Kreuger would tell creditors that he had loaned millions to governments in Europe. To call a note due could cause the collapse of these governments and could lead to war. Creditors were advised to exercise patience.

Kreuger's castle of cards started to tumble when he sold his shares of Erikkson Telephone Company of Sweden to the International Telephone and Telegraph Company of New York. ITT auditors found a "slight" discrepancy in the Erikkson books and an odd connection with Kreuger's Swedish Match Company. When ITT announced termination of merger plans with Erikkson, Kreuger's empire began disintegrating. Swedish bank auditors found his $60 million Italian Treasury Bills, used to back a number of inter-bank loans, were forged. Kreuger ended all speculation about his actions by committing suicide on March 12, 1932. Auditors found that his debts exceeded those of his native Sweden. Still, there were those in Europe and America who

This example of the Ivar Kreuger medal is in the Royal Coin Cabinet in Stockholm

believed the suicide was one more of Kreuger's tricks—that a double had been murdered and the Match King lived out his days in luxury.

Kreuger almost succeeded in one area where all others have failed. He planned a Euro-currency to stabilize the monetary system of Europe. The plan, no longer credited to Kreuger, is still under consideration for Western Europe today. While collectors have no examples of his proposed money, there is an unusual, but scarce, medal available. He gave his friends and business associates gold medals with his portrait on them. In true Ivar Kreuger style, the known examples are in bronze!

A CURRENCY TO BUILD PYRAMIDS

Whenever chain letter promotions or pyramid schemes come to light, the name of Charles Ponzi is invoked. Nineteen eighty-two marked the centennial of the birth in Parma, Italy, of Charles Bianchi, better known to the financial world as Charles Ponzi. His caper involved using money of world postal exchanges—the International Reply Coupon—to raise penny investments to million-dollar profits. At its height in the summer of 1920, Ponzi's operation reportedly took in more than $500,000 per day and paid out $200,000. His promise of "your money back and 50 percent interest in 45 days, or double your money back in 90 days," attracted thousands, including police investigators.

Ponzi's scam had merit. He could have made a legitimate profit had he acted on his scheme and not just talked about it. Instead, Ponzi merely paid old investors with new investors' money. By the time his bubble burst, Ponzi's Security and Exchange Company of Boston had taken more than 30,000 investors for a total of $9.5 million.

In 1906 the Universal Postal Union introduced a coupon currency, the International Reply Coupon. A correspondent in one country could pay for return postage from another. Following World War I, the currency of many European nations was depressed. First class postage in some was no more than a cent or two, while in the

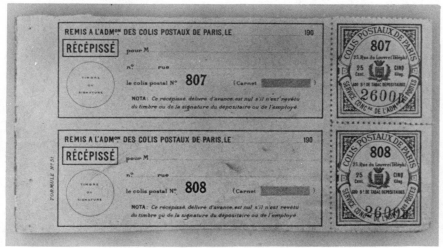

International Reply Coupons

United States, the cost was five cents. The foreign-bought coupons could be exchanged at U.S. post offices and a small profit realized, even discounting the stamps. It is doubtful that Ponzi made more than an initial purchase, just enough to say his scheme was possible.

As a result of Ponzi's game, the price of International Reply Coupons is now set above the highest first-class rate of any Universal Postal Union member. A Ponzi scheme is no longer possible in coupons, but is continually attempted in other areas.

THE MAN WHO WOULD BE SOVEREIGN

Martin Coles Harman was a million-aire whose fantasies included being head of a sovereign state, even if the country was a small island off the English coast. All went well until he decided to make money, half-pennies and pennies, in the unheard of denomination of puffins! But what riled royalty most was that Harman had the audacity to put his own portrait, rather than the king's, on his coinage. The crown had suffered enough. Martin Coles Harman was charged with violating section five of the Coinage Act, 1870.

Lundy is a small island, three miles long by a half-mile wide, near the entrance to the Bristol Channel, but just beyond the twelve-mile limit of the Devonshire coast. The island, not always under British rule, sports a few prehistoric remains and a history of adventure and intrigue. In 1625 it was taken by Turkish pirates; in 1633 by the Spaniards. The French report-edly used it as a base for raids against English shipping. At the time Harman bought the island in 1925, the popula-tion was 45, with a large puffin settlement.

Harman's argument that his claim to the island was stronger than that of the English crown had tenuous merit. He pointed out that no taxes or cus-toms duties had been collected by England and that she had ignored one

Lundy's 1929 fantasy coins are collectors' items

segment of the population when it was attacked and completely annihilated. When pressed for more details by the court as to who died, Harman replied, "the rabbits!" English jurists are not noted for their humor.

As a London financier, Harman had the funds to humor his ego. He paid $88,000 for the island in 1925. Claiming sovereignty, Harman commissioned The Mint—Birmingham, a private corporation, to strike 50,000 bronze pennies and a like number of half-pennies, a sizable quantity considering the total human population of 45. He chose the puffin as his denomination, Harman said, because the bird was very common to the island. The very name of the island, Lundy, meant *puffin* in Icelandic.

During his counterfeiting trial, Harman claimed that Lundy was a "vest-pocket sized, self-governing dominion." Unfortunately, the king's bench failed to agree. Harman was found guilty and fined five pounds, plus court costs of fifteen guineas.

While the English court found Harman's claim illegitimate, collectors feel otherwise about his coins; puffins are now listed in most world coin catalogs. In 1965, with British opposition to tokens lessened, a series of restrikes was issued, more for the tourist and numismatic trade than as a statement of autonomy. The question of sovereignty finally was settled in 1969 when another millionaire, Jack Harwood, purchased the island and gave it to the English people.

A type set of Hutt River coins in a deluxe presentation case

A MAN WITH A GRUDGE

Many people grumble over what they believe to be unjust government interference, but Leonard George Casley did something about it. On April 21, 1970, Casley issued a declaration of secession from the Commonwealth of Australia, claiming his 18,500-acre holding an independent state, to be known as Hutt River Province. Naming himself administrator, he took the title, His Royal Highness Prince Leonard.

The seemingly unjust government act prompting Casley to action was the placing of a limit on the amount of wheat he could harvest on his land. The gross proceeds from the sale of wheat under the new quota would not have paid the interest on the loan he took to purchase two new four-wheel drive tractors. Protests to the government went unanswered. Penalties for violation of the government quota could have included seizure of his lands. Casley saw but one out—secession. Formal notice was served on the government of Western Australia and on the Governor General of Australia. Casley offered the sovereignty of his lands to Her Majesty Queen Elizabeth. Although she declined any acknowledgement, one official did address Casley in government correspondence as, "The Administrator of Hutt River Province," tacit recognition Casley thought.

Hutt, of course, needed its own stamps and money. On October 15, 1973, the Australian Postal Service placed an embargo on all mail addressed to the province. Outbound mail was being delivered under protest, but the material for this story was sent bearing a Hutt River cancellation and using stamps designed solely for use by Prince Leonard. No other postage was placed on the envelope and the material was delivered in the U.S. by our own postal service. Tacit recognition?

The first money issues by Prince Leonard were paper and bore his signature and portrait. A complete set consisted of five notes denominationally colored—ten cents (blue), twenty cents (green), fifty cents (red), one dollar (lavender), and two dollars (brown). All notes were printed on security paper and serially numbered.

In April 1976, Prince Leonard contracted the private Phillips Mint in California to strike an "official" issue of coins. Planned denominations included five-, ten-, twenty- and fifty-cent pieces. Also included was a fine silver thirty-dollar proof coin, and a .900 fine $100 gold piece. Prince Leonard tied his currency to the Australian dollar making it equal to $1.30 U.S. He claimed that he had arranged for his currency to be traded with other nations, but to date the only outside interest in Hutt River coinage has been shown by coin collectors.

THE DUKE FROM DOWN UNDER

As recently as the early 1800s, one of the punishments for counterfeiting in England was transportation to Australia. Today Australia has a few rascals it would like to ship to England. His Grace, The Most Noble, Admiral, Duke of Avram, and Right Honorable Earl of Enoch, must be one. He cannot be charged with counterfeiting for the duke has not copied the currency of the realm. He, like Prince Leonard and other self-proclaimed royalty, simply created his own!

The duke is a modern day Emperor

Norton, without benefit of a broken mind. Nee John Charlton Rudge in 1944, in the Western Australian community of Kalgoorlie, Rudge has always had a creative and promotional bent. Since titles are usually awarded by entities, Rudge created his own—the Duchy of Avram (pronounced AWV-rum)—and awarded himself a number of honors, Knight of the Sword, Royal Knight, Knight of Honour, Chevalier of Honour, Knight of Bountiful Endeavors, to name a few. When he needed money, Rudge printed his own avrams; and when he needed backing for the currency, he created his own bank, The Royal Bank of Avram.

The Duke of Avram's regalia and royal pretensions have given fodder to the tabloids down under. He grants audiences and likes interviews. The headlines serve his purposes: *Amazing, Your Grace; Tasmanian Businessman Finds Way To Make A Million, He Prints His Own!*

What possesses a man to call his neighbors his *subjects*; his neighborhood a *duchy*; his modest family home on the banks of the Tamar River a

Face and back of the twenty-five-avram commemorative note issued for the wedding of Prince Charles and Lady Diana

dukery; his wife *Her Grace, the Duchess of Avram*; his two daughters *the Ladies Rudge*; and his son *Lord Charles, Marquis of Mathra*?

A clue may lie in the currency he issues. The duke claims that there are more than one million avrams in circulation today (200,000 $ Australian). His grace's currency is avrams (AWV-rums) and ducals (DEW-shuls), the latter being one-hundredth of an avram. He hand signs all his notes, which come in denominations of one, three, five, seven and fifteen avrams. The duke is planning a coinage issue with his portrait, and his coins will be in denominations of one-, three-, seven-, fifteen-, thirty- and seventy-five-ducals. The duke sells his currency to collectors at face, but face is $3.60 (U.S.) to one avram.

There is one commemorative note, too, issued by the duke for the wedding of Prince Charles and Lady Di. Avram sent a specimen of the twenty-five avram note to the royal couple as a wedding gift!

The duke claims his monetary system is legal, but advises subjects using avrams not to just walk into a shop and try to cash them. Subjects might end up where the Australia government would like to put the duke.

His Grace, The Most Noble, Admiral, Duke of Avram, and Right Honorable Earl of Enoch

THE CURRENCY OF A FANTASY ISLAND

We all remember the tale of the Three Little Pigs from childhood. When the wolf was at the door and begged, "little pig, little pig, let me come in," the porcine response was, "No, not by the hair of my chinny chin chin!" Near Lyons, France, the hair of the chinny chin chin appertains to another fantasy. It is the denominational value of currency from Beard Island!

Lyons is a city of year-round Mardi Gras. It has its industries and businesses, but it is a city of fantasy, trying very hard not to take itself too seriously. Lyons is also a city *gastronomique* claiming the greatest chefs of France. Only a Lyonnaise could take an island, a restaurant, and the hair from a chinny chin chin and create an acceptable fantasy.

Ile Barbe is a small wooded island in the River Saone, on the northern outskirts of the city. In Roman times it was called Insula Barabara and over the centuries verbal shorthand has cut the name to Ile Barbe. This well suits the Lyonnaise humor for the name translates to Beard Island!

It was Felix Benoit, writer and humorist, who declared Ile Barbe independent and called himself Don Felix I; the historic date, March 16, 1977. J.L. Ansanay-Alex, sole resident and proprietor of L'Auberge de l'Ile, a famous restaurant on the island, was in full agreement. The

The punishment for counterfeiting Ile Barbe notes is to lose one's arms!

citizens of Lyons had a laugh, the press a field day.

Diplomatic recognition was slow in materializing, but anticipating the "inevitable," Don Felix I named consuls to represent him. There are Ile Barbe consulates in the United States, The Netherlands, Great Britain, Canada and Sweden. Coincidentally most consular officers are stamp dealers, for Ile Barbe has issued 113 different stamps, twenty souvenir blocks, one fiscal stamp, and for its consular mail, thirteen special stamps. In addition, Ile Barbe caters to the philatelic specialist with creations of overprints, errors, and other varieties. Values are in the island currency—poils—which the linguist will recognize is French for "hairs," most appropriate for Beard Island.

Beard Island currency is in one-quarter-, one-half-, and one-poil notes. If you were to visit the restaurant on Ile Barbe, you could pay in island currency, but you'd not be pulling any hairs from J.L. Ansanay-Alex's chinny chin chin. The rate of exchange is $2.00 U.S. to one hair!

HIS MONEY WAS FOR THE BIRDS

In May of 1982, the undeclared war in the Falklands dominated the British press. Each agonizing step was broadcast, televised and headlined. Each island, town, port, hamlet and settlement was mentioned by name— save one, the Jason Islands group. Perhaps the fact that all inhabitants but a caretaker were penguins and albatrosses contributed to the omission.

WEST FALKLAND

Jason Islands

Port Egmont

Roy Cove · Port Howard

King George Bay

Queen Charlotte Bay

Weddell Jsl.

·Chartres

Goose Green

Falkland Sound

Fox Bay

North Arm

Bay of H

61° 60°W.

The Jason Islands are an archipelago stretching northwest from West Falkland

Islands in the Jason group in 1970 to found a bird sanctuary. To help underwrite the $11,000 costs for the islands, Hill issued his own "money" and "postage stamps." The sale to collectors helped maintain the wildlife refuge. Unfortunately, Hill died suddenly in December 1981 having just returned from the Falklands.

Hill claimed his money to be legal tender on the Jasons and since no one lived there, the validity of the currency was never challenged. His notes were issued in denominations of fifty pence, one-, five-, ten-, and twenty-pounds. Though the sizes and colors changed with the values, the format remained the same: a portrait of Hill to the right and a different penguin to the left—Humboldt, Jackass, Rockhopper, Gentoo, or King, depending upon the denomination. For the Conservation Year of 1970, Hill also issued a two-shilling postage stamp. Since neither penguins nor albatrosses write, no cancelled version of the stamp exists.

It was not the Argentine invasion of the Falklands, but the death of Leonard W. Hill, that brought the dream of Jason Island's currency to an end. The islands are a bird sanctuary. The currency was "issued" to raise funds for the property.

Leonard Hill, known as the "Penguin Millionaire," was the director of the Birdland Zoo Gardens, Bourton-on-the-Water, Gloucestershire. A member of the Federation of Zoological Gardens of Great Britain and Ireland, Hill bought Grand and Steeple

Uninhabited, the Jason Island currency was issued to raise funds for a bird sanctuary in the Falklands

UNCOMMON TALES OF COMMON COUNTERFEITERS -- Part I

THE MINT AT MONROE

Treasury records indicate 47 million five-cent pieces were coined bearing the date 1927: 37 million at Philadelphia, 5.7 million at Denver, and 3.4 million at San Francisco. Official Mint records completely overlook the production of a small mint in downstate New York. It's production rivaled that of the Denver Mint and nearly doubled that of San Francisco. Mint record keepers can be forgiven. The five million 1927 five-cent pieces struck at the Monroe mint were not coined until late 1934 and early 1935!

This revised count, not reflected in numismatic records, combines United States Secret Service figures with the Treasury count. The mint at Monroe may have been cost-efficient, but it was not legal. The coins were counterfeit and a plague to government agents in five states—New York, New Jersey, Connecticut, Pennsylvania and Delaware. Secret Service agents searched furtively for a year for the source of counterfeit nickels.

In 1934 it was worth a counterfeiter's time to fake nickels. A nickel would buy a cup of coffee, two doughnuts, even a hamburger. Five cents was a third of an hour's labor, if one even had a job; this was the time of the Great Depression. It was also the shirttail period of another era—Prohibition. The combination led to the discovery of the mint at Monroe.

It was a Saturday morning in 1935,

The Monroe mint's production of 1927 Buffalo equaled that of the Denver Mint

colder than usual, even for New York in early March. Police, searching the deep woods near an abandoned farm in Chester, stumbled upon a pipe protruding from the ground. Thinking he had discovered an illicit still, Sgt. George Consilia from the State Police barracks at Monroe, put his ear to the pipe and detected the faint chug of a gasoline engine. Investigating further, he and trooper William Meischburger found the ruins of an old farmhouse nearby. The next morning, a surprise raid reinforced with T-agents and troopers, netted a completely equipped mint and led to the arrest of three men—brothers Louis and George Ehlers, and Leo Gailie.

The mint site was like the ruins of a movie set: collapsed roof, fallen doors and walls, broken windows. But an indistinct path through the rubble led to a cellar housing a completely outfitted machine shop, stamping press, boxes of blank planchets, 3,400 finished 1927 Buffalo nickels and a sizeable quantity of raw metal. The coins were distributed through a mini-Federal system—the "bankers" paid fifty cents on the dollar face for the coins, which netted a profit of two cents per coin, after discount.

THE CHICAGO MONEY MACHINE CAPER

It is midsummer, 1929. The stock market crash is three months away, and everyone is rushing headlong to invest in the market; no stock is difficult to sell. The stage is set for a small group that has concocted a scheme to sell stock in a "machine" that makes money, a sort of do-it-yourself BEP.

The schemers include Howard Ward, Joseph Yerkes, John Dobbins, Harry Robinson and J.E. Dewey.

Leading the operation is a twenty-year veteran of the Chicago Police Department, Sgt. William Begley. Together they build their first money machine—a small, wooden box with slots at either end that "transforms" one-dollar bills into one-hundred dollar bills. Soon they have their first investor; cabinet maker Jean B. Hassewer invests $1,000.

Before the prototype money machine can be manufactured in quantity, refinements must be made. A timer must be installed, allowing the production of no more than one bill per hour. Ostensibly, this gives the "chemicals" time to erase the printing on the one-dollar bills and allows the ink to dry on the new one-hundred-dollar bills. But, as one member of the company candidly mused, the timer "gives us time to get away before the rube discovers the scam!"

What the group possesses in imagination, it lacks in mechanical skill and soon Hassewer's initial investment is gone. Begley then has an idea, that will not only quiet Hassewer but will elicit more money from him. They tell him that the scheme has been discovered by Federal agents. As an investor, he is as involved as the rest, but with Begley's connections, a little money will "fix the case." Hassewer hands over another $1,000.

The confidence game has now grown into extortion, and the schemers become greedier. They ask another $500 of Hassewer, depleting the last of his savings. Reluctantly he goes to the state's attorney's office, confesses his involvement, and a trap is set for the con men. Detectives hide in the cabinet maker's shop to witness Hassewer's last payment. On the unconscious body of Officer Begley, who was beaten "resisting arrest"

the detectives discover the marked money.

Tragically, the final chapter of this story is yet to come. On January 7, 1930, six months after his confession, Jean B. Hassewer is found shot to death on the steps of his Chicago apartment. As the coroner notes, "There's little question that he paid with his life for exposing the swindle."

THE MINTMASTER OF CHICAGO

Harry Kritzke fit the grandfather description perfectly—in his early sixties, polite, mild mannered, with a constant twinkle in his eye. He had a quick wit, loved good books and had an extensive reference library. But, Harry Kritzke hated to spend money—the real kind.

Kritzke's search for good books proved expensive, even in mid-Depression years, so to support his hobby, he maintained three independent sources of income: he had a small rental income, drew a weekly welfare check as a "destitute," and operated his own mint.

The Chicago bibliophile's private mint was located in his own building, rent free. The mint was not a simple affair. Heavy machinery included a stamping press, drills and lathes of the finest sort. Kritzke limited production to half-dollars and quarters, die-stamped in base metal and silver dipped to camouflage the leaden appearance. His products were described as "excellent." Kritzke had been a machinist before he "retired."

The discovery of Kritzke's operation was accidental. Tendering one of his home produced half-dollars to pay for a cold beer on a sultry afternoon, Kritzke dropped the coin on the bar rather than easing it down. A nearby

Secret Service agent recognized the odd sound of the coins on the hard surface.

Kritzke was searched and found to be carrying several pieces of homemade money. A subsequent search of his library revealed volumes on astrology, botany, chemistry, electrical engineering, mathematics, metal sciences and moral philosophy; *and* his well-equipped, but very unauthorized mint!

THE MAN WHO MADE HIS OWN

"I see one-third of a nation illhoused, ill-clad, ill-nourished," said Franklin Delano Roosevelt in a 1937 Presidential address to the nation. Edward Mueller, retired from managing an apartment block of New York's East Side was among that third. The United States Supreme Court had just upheld the Social Security Act, but Mueller was not eligible. He had to fend for himself.

Edward Mueller's needs were modest. He was a widower, lived in an inexpensive apartment on 96th Street, was not a big eater. The only other mouth he had to feed was his dog's. He could have lived with his married daughter, but Edward Mueller was an independent man. His mind was alert, sharp, and full of ideas. One day, promenading his dog, Mueller spotted an old hand-fed press in a used goods store and saw there the answer to his future.

Mueller's new equipment was too small for most needs, but it was just right for him. With it, he could solve the problem of income for his retirement years. When he tended the apartment houses on the East Side, Mueller dabbled in photography. He had a camera, knew how to develop film and print negatives.

Mueller took one of his few remaining dollars and photographed it. With a few familiar chemicals, he etched metal plates for the front and back of his dollar bill. No matter that he did not have the right kind of paper, nor that he even had the right kind or shade of green ink. "Who looks at dollar bills," he thought, justifyingly?

The former caretaker had always lived a simple life and was not about to change. He never wanted for more than a dollar or two a day, so he never printed more than he needed, nor would he ever cash more than one bill at any given establishment. When a purchase exceeded two dollars, only one of the notes tendered would be of his apartment manufacture.

The old man's dollars were later described as "extremely crude," so bad that no one should have been fooled. When the ink would dry and cake on his plates, Mueller would simply add more ink. The condition of his printing plates further deteriorated with his age. Still, no one caught him or challenged his notes, at least not on his tendering them. His production was now starting to amount to a sizable sum; the Secret Service held more than 6,000 examples of his money. Agents were baffled; they were as angry at those who accepted such obviously fake money, as they were with the unknown criminal producing them.

The day of reckoning dawned for Edward Mueller quite by accident. While he was out walking his dog and cashing his daily note, there was a fire in his apartment. Firemen tried to salvage his meagre belongings by throwing them out the window—press, counterfeit notes, all. A curious passerby helped himself to a sample and when Mueller returned, he found a reception committee of city detectives.

Secret Service agents were chagrined that his solitary little old man was the "gang of counterfeiters" they had been hunting for the past decade. Mueller was tried, convicted and sentenced to nine months for his malefactoring. On his release he was forced to give up his apartment, his press, his camera, and finish his days with his daughter and son-in-law.

Author's note: The Secret Service has been very cooperative in most instances, but Edward Mueller was apparently such an embarrassment that the Service has ignored requests for material for this story. They must prefer not to remember Edward Mueller.

THE CASE OF THE INNOCENT COUNTERFEITER

When Rev. James R. Kaye decided to make award medals to help stimulate attendance at his Sunday school classes, he discovered how difficult early twentieth century counterfeit laws could be. His timing coincided with the introduction of a newly designed cent commemorating the centennial of the birth of the sixteenth President. Kaye's Presbyterian church was located in the central Illinois town bearing that President's name—Lincoln.

Reverend Kaye's sole idea was to induce children to study their bible lessons. Funds were short, so perhaps, he thought, he could make the medals himself. He never dreamed of doing anything illegal.

Using new coins as model masters, Reverend Kaye tried making plaster molds, but his mechanical abilities failed to match his imagination.

Abandoning his project, he discarded the plaster molds in the nearest trash bin. Pastor Kaye never dreamed he was setting the stage for the nightmare that followed.

His practice molds were discovered, government agents notified and the Illinois minister was charged with violating statutes relating to the counterfeiting laws of the United States! Logic abandoned, the Presbyterian minister was tried twice and found guilty on both occasions. He was given first a two-year prison term; lack of intent to defraud mattered not. He appealed, and the second time the judge displayed a hint of leniency. This time Kaye was sentenced to six months in the Peoria House of Corrections.

Word of the pastor's predicament reached the White House. President William Howard Taft, noting that Reverend Kaye never intended to duplicate U.S. coins, gave him a Presidential pardon. The date of the President's edict was July 17, 1910, two days before Rev. Kaye would complete his full term at Peoria.

President Taft was in a benevolent mood the day he pardoned the minister. Included in the same writ of clemency was Frank Minor, pardoned after completing twenty-seven years of a life sentence for the murder of his wife; and Esias Willie, convicted for murder in Indian Territory. Rev. James R. Kaye was in infamous company.

EVERY CASE IS A "BIG" CASE

Many of Secret Service division chief William F. Flynn's counterfeiting cases seem to have a familiar ring. At interviews following an arrest, the chief is likely to tell reporters a repetitive tale: "The most skillful counterfeiters ever caught,'' or the culprits operate ''the most elaborate'' or the ''best equipped'' plant he has ever seen. The bad coins ''flood the East Coast,'' and, ''only a trained person can detect the bad money.''

With Flynn, no arrest is an ordinary arrest. Either New York's coin casters are among the most sophisticated in the world, or the Secret Service chief relishes the limelight. New York reporters are very obliging. The case of Guiseppe Pisantano and Ignazio Cecala is no exception.

The date is Saturday, December 11, 1912. Flynn reports the two men he has just apprehended are thought to have flooded the eastern and New England states with bad money.

''After weeks of watching, I succeeded yesterday in catching two Sicilians at work. They are the most skillful counterfeiters of silver money ever caught in this country. They live at 230 Chrystie street. In a flat on the fourth floor of this tenement, they have a 'mint,' where they coined fifty-, twenty-five-, and ten-cent pieces. When captured the pair had ready for distribution some 7,000 coins. The plant in which the coins were made is very elaborate; only a person trained in detecting bad money could tell the coins were not genuine.''

For more than a month agents have been trying to find the source of spurious counterfeit coins circulating in the east, particularly New England. Ten days ago, Flynn's agents crossed the trail of Pisantano and Cecala and the two were kept under twenty-four hour surveillance. When Flynn accumulated sufficient evidence, he led his men on a raid of the ''mint.''

Early yesterday morning, Flynn posted men on the street in front of the tenement, on the roofs of adjoining buildings, and in the back yards of the tenements. He was taking no chances. With two more men, Chief Flynn headed up the back stairs to the suspected private mint. At the fourth floor he paused, thinking he detected the ''tinkle of coins.'' As he was about to knock, he noticed a peephole. Peering in, he found himself eyeball to to an eyeball ''as black as coal.''

Flynn gave the order to break in. In a few seconds they were in the apartment and found Pisantano and Cecala cowering in a back room. On a table were 7,000 shiny new coins. Flynn signaled the agents in the street and on the roof tops to join him. They found a dozen melting pots, forty molds, and ''some of the best dies ever seen used by counterfeiters.''

Caught red-handed, Pisantano and Cecala offered a novel, but fruitless defense. Their plea—not guilty! The

Counterfeit coin sold for thirty-five cents on the dollar

pair explained to the judge that they were making money for their "personal use" but the judge would not buy their alibi any more than he would their money—which they sold for thirty-five cents on the real dollar. Pisantano and Cecala are held in lieu of bail of $7,500 each (in genuine money).

Upon parting, Flynn compliments the pair, "I have never seen a finer layout of its kind than this one!"

TOO HOT TO HANDLE

Secret Service agent Otto Klinke was beginning to wonder if all the money in circulation was being made in the New York City area. He had permanent scars to remind him of his latest caper. Two weeks earlier, Klinke had participated in a raid on a Long Island mansion to apprehend gold coin fabricators Franz Webber and Benjamin Lotterer. Now, barely a fortnight later, Klinke and partner Joseph Wishart closed down another home mint, this one producing a complete line of silver coins, from the dime to the dollar. The December 27, 1910, midnight raid was on a house at 78 Johnson Avenue, in New York's Williamsburg section and followed the arrest of Frank Spielberg, earlier in the evening. Spielberg confessed to being a counterfeiter after agents found a pocketful of incriminating coins on him.

Spielberg led Government agents to his plant at the Johnson Avenue address—a two-story building overshadowed by a six-story tenement building in front. Spielberg rapped hard on the front door, hoping his partner would remember knocking was to be answered at the rear door only. Partner Jacob Droos apparently forgot and cracked open the door. Agent Klinke pushed his way in, surprising

Droos who was holding a ladle filled with molten metal. Klinke was equally surprised when Droos handed him the ladle—hot end first!

Despite the smell of his own burned flesh mingling with that of molten metal, Klinke barged in to find a stove for melting, several molds, a number of coolers for hardening the coins, and $4,000 in a mixture of silver denominations, as well as a quantity of base metal. After securing first-aid for his hand, and securing Droos and Spielberg in jail, Klinke found that the two had served their counterfeiting apprenticeship in Russia, before graduation to the U.S. a year earlier. The counterfeiters distributed their money through pushcart peddlers in Manhattan and Brooklyn, wholesaling $1,000 lots for $600. None of their coins were faulted in circulation; only later when Manhattan banks prepared to recirculate them.

THE MYSTERY OF THE TIMES SQUARE COUNTERFEITS

Christmas is a time, according to law enforcement officials, when the passers of bad paper—checks and bills—are busiest. During the Depression years, bad coins were as prevalent as bad paper.

A few days after Christmas, 1934, a flow of complaints begins to reach the desk of Allen G. Straight, head of the Secret Service in New York. The city is being inundated with counterfeit quarters, particularly around midtown Manhattan—Times Square, 42nd Street and Eighth Avenue. Straight calls special agent James Veary to investigate.

Hugh Mulvey, an Eighth Avenue subway agent, is one of the first to be interviewed. "Do I get bad quarters?

Well, I should say I do," responds Mulvey in a heavy Irish brogue. "I get a batch of them every day. Some days I get as many as thirty." He adds, "For the last three months they have been coming in, but I manage to spot them. Yes, I do."

Frank Ledwith, another Eighth Avenue subway agent, confirms Mulvey's report, "I get five or six a day. They're older coins." D.C. O'Connor, I.R.T. change booth agent in Times Square tells Veary that he refuses many quarters each day.

The story is little different at the United Cigar store. No one there has a spurious quarter for the Government agent. Veary reports back to his chief.

"We can't get a prosecution without evidence. I want to *see* one of those phony coins," orders the New York Secret Service head. Obligingly, Mulvey puts aside a few coins for Straight.

"As I suspected!" exclaims Straight in a most Sherlock Holmes pose. "These are the Victory type and they're genuine! Look, says the government officer to agent Veary, Look closely," he says to Veary. "The date on these coins is simply worn off. They were designed that way."*

Collectors recognize the quarters as the Standing Liberty design issued from 1916 to 1930. Because of constant complaint of date wear, mint engravers made minor modifications in the design in 1925. The date appears on the obverse, at the base of the pedestal on which Miss Liberty stands. In 1925 the date was set deeper, protected by the rest of the design. Prior to the surgical corrections, the date was the high point, wearing after brief circulation. Collectors, aware of the scarcity of collectible quarters from 1916 to 1924, have always paid a premium for dated specimens.

Although it had been only a few years since the new Washington quarter was introduced, rumors abounded in New York of coins believed to be fakes. How many dateless Standing Liberty coins were thrown away by frightened citizens who thought them counterfeit?

The date wore easily on many Liberty Standing quarters

THE WOODCHOPPERS' NICKELS

The year was 1909. Theodore Roosevelt was President of the United States. Five-cent pieces in circulation were primarily Liberty head or V-nickels, depending on where one lived. New Englanders and New Yorkers preferred V-nickels, while the rest of the country used the term Liberty head. Since five cents was a fair portion of one's hourly wage, it was not surprising that nickels were counterfeited. Their plain edges, with no reeding to worry about, made five-cent pieces easier to fake than dimes or quarters.

When reports of fake nickels reached Secret Service agents, they acted with the same diligence as if the coins had been gold pieces. But when reports indicated that the fake coins emanated from a socially prominent neighborhood, the agents acted with extreme diligence.

The bad coins were traced to the estate of H.J. Roosevelt, cousin of the

President. Fortunately, investigations showed that Roosevelt was totally unaware that his Long Island estate harbored a private mint, and was not implicated.

Secret Service agents Callihan and Rubano were assigned to the case. Arrested were Guiseppe Bava and Domenico Pugiliese, woodchoppers in Roosevelt's employ. They were charged with the counterfeiting of five-cent pieces and the agents found a quantity of bad nickels hidden in the hut where the men slept.

The arrest was not what one would call "textbook." As Rubano's name implied, he was Italian, which gave him a distinctive advantage over Callihan. Rubano's fluent Italian probably saved his life and that of his partner.

As Bava and Pugiliese reluctantly led the federal agents to their hut, accompanied by the entire force of woodchoppers, they plotted to overcome their captors at the first opportunity. Unaware that Rubano understood every word, the woodcutters conspired to grab whatever would come in handy and "make way" with the agents.

Surprise being the best element of a good fight, Callihan and Rubano charged the woodchoppers, and before they realized what was happening, they were manacled together. Bava and Pugiliese were armed, one carrying a revolver and the other a stiletto. They were committed to New

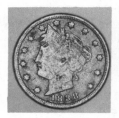

The Woodchopper's Nickels

Raymond Street jail and held in lieu of bail. Their cohorts, five other woodcutters, were released.

THE EASY MONEY OF THE PROMISED NEW LAND

The plight of poor emigrants venturing to America is not new. In the late nineteenth and early twentieth centuries, more than ten million ventured to the new world, many riding "steerage" in the bowels of dilapidated and slow sailing ships. The voyage across the Atlantic could last several weeks, but few had the good fortune to secure bunk space—wooden planks laddered four high along the bulkheads. Most slept directly on the lower decks, bedded in scant straw often soiled by seasickness on prior voyages. Below water level, there were no portholes for ventilation. Meal service was nonexistent, the emigrants preparing their own and often waiting long hours for their turn in the small galleys. A few went mad; others died. But a few, at least, passed the time scheming.

Most of the emigrants were escaping the poverty of their homelands for the promise of something better in America. Their scant supply of money was hoarded; a promise of stretching it a little, to obtain money of the new country at a discount, was what America was all about. When the *Koenig Albert* of the North German Lloyd Line bound from Italy, docked in New York in early June 1909 and discharged her 814 steerage passengers, most had in their possession, quantities of United States half-dollars, all counterfeit.

The U.S. Immigration Bureau and the Secret Service were investigating a band of counterfeiters who distributed through agents in Italy when the

Koenig Albert docked. Europeans distrusted paper money. Warned about the "funny money" offered at discount, they began to shun the bargains and the counterfeiters turned to "silver" money.

Investigation revealed how the counterfeiters had cut their foreign distributors from the scam and had saved shipping charges to Italy, along with agents' commissions. Boarding the *Koenig Albert* at Hoboken, they flimflammed the newcomers out of the legal tender they had left. Not only did the emigrants lose their meagre savings, they were held further at Ellis Island while authorities investigated those who usurped the privileges of the Treasury.

Cast copy of a Barber half-dollar

WHAT'S A MOTHER TO DO?

The meaning of English novelist Edward George Bulwer-Lytton's words, *Nature's loving proxy, the watchful mother*, was never more meaningful than the time maternal instinct drove a New York woman to write police inspector Bolan, "A gang of young men has been trying to induce my son, who is a conductor on the Second Avenue surface line, to distribute counterfeit nickels to passengers. The counterfeiters are in a house on East 107th Street."

The mother's concern coincided with complaints from shopkeepers in the neighborhood, reporting that they had been hoodwinked into giving good dollars in exchange for bad nickels. The passers of the bogus money made small purchases, engaged the shopkeepers in small talk, and then asked for a small favor—exchange of their bulky hoard of change for a bill or two.

In the second scam revealed by the watchful mother, trolleymen co-mingled good and bad change to passengers. The letter provided the clue police needed to narrow their investigation.

Early in October 1915, inspector Bolan assigned NYPD detective Caspers and policeman Gisselboch to a neighborhood stakeout near the east side of Second Avenue, close to 107th Street. Gisselboch guarded the rear exit while Caspers rushed the front door, raced the stairs and forced open a door on an upper floor. As Caspers burst into the room, two revolvers fell or were thrown out the window, narrowly missing Gisselboch, stationed below.

Five men were apprehended in the raid. A search of the coin den revealed that production was limited to five-cent pieces. Detective Caspers' inventory of seized material listed one melting pot, one mold and two bad nickels. Four of the five captured men were trolley car conductors. Two were released and two—Frank Sceanto and Frank Gullimo—were arrested. Booked with them was Michael Laconte, a driver. Each was held on $1,000 bail. Only then were federal authorities notified and the small mint with limited production closeu.

A spurious 1902 Liberty head nickel

A BAD PENNY MAKER ALWAYS GETS TURNED IN

To think of counterfeiting one-cent pieces is an attack on logic. Government agents found it equally incredible. As of August 17, 1909, the Treasury Department was aware of only one instance when bad pennies were made for circulation.

During late spring and early summer 1909, reports claimed confectionery stores, corner groceries and neighborhood taverns in Brooklyn's eastern section were being inundated with spurious cents. So concerned was the Government that three of its top agents were assigned to track the counterfeiter with seemingly high production but low ambition.

Secret Service agents Costange, Klinke and Schroeder followed the bad cent trail that ultimately led to two counterfeiters, Augustino Suriano and Bernard Vecchio. It was soon apparent why the pair selected cents to copy. Both men were molders employed by White's Brass Foundry, located in Brooklyn's industrial section at North Third and Berry Streets. The company had been without a foundry foreman for several months, and Suriano and Vecchio were reported to have taken advantage of the situation by trying their hands at a little free enterprise. They turned the company's time and its brass material into copper-colored one-cent pieces for themselves!

IN ANTICIPATION OF THE CHRISTMAS RUSH

Today, if Government agents were to raid a shop and find men sitting at benches polishing coins, chances are the men would be *whizzers*, trying to make circulated coins look better for the numismatic investors' market. But in 1909, condition grading meant little to the collector-investor. Coins were polished to make them look real, not better.

On December 16, 1909, United States Secret Service agents raided a New York City counterfeiting plant in full operation. Three men were seated at benches polishing newly "minted" fifty-cent pieces. On a table nearby was a hot melting pot.

The men were booked into Manhattan's Oak Street Station as James O'Brien, Alvin Clark and George Costello. The names were as phony as the fifty half-dollars they had been polishing.

Secret Service chief William J. Flynn identified the enterprising trio as John "Curly" Fanning (who had already served one prison term for counterfeiting); Alvin Caplin and George Carlo. Their mint, geared for quantity production, was located in the rear of a flat at 129 East 144th Street in uptown Manhattan. Government agents found a half dozen melting pots, six to eight molds, a silver plating outfit, a "considerable" quantity of metal, polishes and other essentials for making cheap money for the Christmas rush.

A bad penny—1859 Indian head cent

A privately made
half-dollar
dated 1907

IN GOD WE TRUST HE UNDERSTANDS

As a youth, it seemed that church ushers often played Sunday morning dictator. They took it personally if nothing was put in their collection basket; being broke was no excuse.

One Sunday morning, so long ago that the year best be forgotten, the collection basket stopped in front of me. Looking to the usher for compassion was fruitless. His stern glare returned the message from Corinthians: *God loveth a cheerful giver*.

Zippers were not yet standard equipment on pants. Inspiration, a quick yank, and a silver-colored, coin-sized button plopped into the collection basket accompanied by a thought from the Old Testament, *if thou have but a little, be not afraid to give according to that little*.

In the early 1900's, New York vestry men faced a crisis that led them first to their congregations and later to Federal authorities. Counterfeit coins in the collection plate were becoming a problem. Hesitant to accuse their parishioners, churchmen did suspect that some saw this as a way to discharge their Sunday obligations while disposing of their bad money.

Were churchgoers becoming less conscientious about passing spurious coin in the house of God? Authorities thought not, that the improved skill of the counterfeiter had instead made it harder to detect the true character of the change.

Today few coins—good or bad—make it to the collection plate. Inflation, prosperity, conscience, all dictate the use of folding money.

The collection plate special—a poorly cast dime

CUPID PUTS AN END TO THE TENTH STREET MINT

It is Spring, 1916. John Kupic is young, impetuous and in love. The object of his dreams is pretty Rose Somday, a neighbor living in the same Tenth Street apartment building in Passaic, New Jersey. The morning is bright and John is cheerful, whistling as he skips down the stairs. He passes Rose's door, stops, and, in an irresistible moment, bursts into her apartment. "Rose," he pleads, "Why can't you love me. I have loads of money and we could be happy together." And then Kupic plants a kiss full upon her lips.

Rose is not impressed. She screams and a passing patrolman, John Callahan, bounds up the stone steps, through the vestibule doors, to answer the young lady's call of distress. Kupic hightails up the next flight of stairs to his own apartment, Officer Callahan just a few steps behind.

Callahan questions the young man and searches his apartment. John

Kupic fibbed not to Rose Somday. He does have "loads of money"—a trunk full of silver dollars, all counterfeit! Kupic also has all the paraphernalia necessary to make more money when his current supply is exhausted.

Kupic is arrested and scheduled to appear before Passaic city court judge Thomas P. Costello. Kupic pleads guilty to a charge of annoying Miss Somday. "I only wanted to kiss her," he tells the judge.

Kupic denies ownership of the counterfeit cartwheels, claiming, "A friend of mine, who is a collector, gave it all to me."

Judge Costello does not believe Kupic any more than Miss Somday did. He is remanded to Federal authorities to face counterfeiting charges.

Cupid's silver dollar—1890-O

SIXTEEN QUARTERS TO THE DOLLAR

More than thirty years had passed since Paolo Aiello immigrated to the United States from Italy, yet he still had not learned the language of his adopted country. There was little need. Since his arrival in 1905, Aiello had not left New York's lower east side, the "Little Italy" of the new world. Paolo sold Italian language church hymnals and Bibles to fellow immigrants. Many times he complained that this was not an easy way to sustain a wife, a stepdaughter and himself. So he felt no guilt each week when he took a day out from Bible selling to stand in line to collect the fifteen-dollar weekly stipend from New York City's Home Relief Bureau for being "unemployed."

Frugal Aiello was eventually able to buy an old car. This was his warehouse, storefront and office for the church hymnal and Bible business. Forever enterprising, the little Italian stretched his income even further by making the change he made change with, or so it was said.

The Depression years kept Secret Service agents busy seeking counterfeiters in America's larger cities. In New York, far too many bogus Standing Liberty quarters plagued merchants, for Treasury officials not to be concerned. The coins were well made, often changing hands through several transactions before being discovered.

The Secret Service assigned agent Peter Rubano to the case of the bogus quarters circulating in Little Italy. Italian himself, Rubano spoke the street dialect. It was Aiello's misfortune when the Government agent tendered a dollar bill to purchase a hymnal. Rubano responded to the book peddler's change with, "You're under arrest!"

Agent Rubano reported finding forty dollars worth of spurious quarters in a compartment under the rear seat of Aiello's car. The coins were wrapped in officious looking packets, not unlike bank rolls. The agent also itemized Aiello's inventory—1 Bible, 15 hymnals, 1 squash, 2 melons, a quantity of peanuts, and a woman's bathing suit. A search failed to reveal the source of Aiello's change.

Arraigned before a United States commissioner, Aiello pleaded, "I am the father of seven sons." But his nemesis Rubano informed the commissioner that all seven sons were from a previous marriage, grown, with families of their own. "And," added the Treasury agent, "He's a second offender."

The commissioner was not moved by the Bible seller's plea. Aiello's bail was set at $4,000. Court calendars, less crowded than today's, allowed justice to move swiftly. On August 19, 1935, less than a month after his arrest, Aiello was sentenced to eighteen months in jail. He pleaded guilty to the charge of possessing 160 counterfeit quarters, but maintained he bought them from an unnamed source at the price of four fakes for one genuine.

Sixteen cast quarters to the real dollar

TENNESSEE'S BARS AND STRIPES MINT

Often, when a convict has time on his hands, his genius can rival that of Edison, Westinghouse, or Ford. Sam Howerton had all but given up hope of escape or release. He was confined to a maximum security cell in the Tennessee State Prison at Nashville, serving his sentence for murder.

Howerton's goal was not lofty: just a little spending money for an occasional cigarette or candy bar. But there was little way to earn spending money in prison in 1913, so Howerton concentrated on making his own.

The prison workshop proved source rich—a little plaster of Paris, scraps of solder, pieces of electric wire, a flat piece of metal, and Howerton had the workings of a modest mint. Sam Howerton never dreamed of wealth; he only wanted a little pocket change.

By means of a wire attached to the electric outlet in his cell, the prisoner fashioned a way to melt the solder, but his trial dies left much to be desired. Howerton hid his plaster molds as he pondered how to improve his product. Regrettably, prisons harbor many obstacles to progress. One that Howerton overlooked was the stool pigeon. A fellow inmate, perhaps out of jealousy, reported the would-be coin maker and that brought an end to the mint in the Tennessee State Prison.

DANVILLE'S FORGOTTEN CITIZEN

Danville, Illinois' main claim to fame is that Abraham Lincoln slept there. On Gilbert Street, the Vermilion County Museum features period furniture from the homes of prominent townsfolk in nineteenth and twentieth

60

century settings. Dr. Fithian's dental office appears as it did to anxious patients back in 1914. But, there is nothing of Charles E. Brown.

In 1908, Brown was prominent—socially and professionally. There were those who felt the thirty-five-year-old attorney would enter politics someday. He had an attractive wife, a three-year-old child, seemingly everything, but he wanted more. Money was a particular quest. If he could not make it fast enough with a good law practice, perhaps he could speed things up by making it in his basement.

Danville residents were shocked on the morning of July 11, 1908, to learn that the previous day, Secret Service agents descended on their town and, in the presence of Brown's wife and child, arrested him on charges of counterfeiting. In Brown's desk in the cellar, Government agents found a complete counterfeiting plant, ready, they said, to begin the manufacture of five-dollar gold pieces, half-dollars, quarters, dimes, even five-cent pieces.

SILVER HAD A TARNISHED NAME

His name was Silver; his game, pot metal—lots of it. When United States Secret Service agents arrested Max Silver, they uncovered the largest cache of counterfeit coins taken in a single raid—seven thousand dimes, one thousand quarters and sixty molds.

Silver operated a cigar store and newsstand in New York City, at 688 Tenth Avenue. His business provided an easy outlet for comingling spurious coins with legitimate change.

Base metal, cast copies of the dimes and quarters in circulation during the early part of the twentieth century were not Max Silver's only coin interests. Arrested with Silver on December 29, 1910, was a jeweler known as "Gorum," David Bartesky on the police blotter, who operated a jewelry store at 234 Second Street. Together they were charged with having in their possession, steel dies for striking spurious Russian gold roubles, a favored bullion piece of Jewish immigrants of the time!

UNCOMMON TALES OF COMMON COUNTERFEITERS -- Part II

THE LADIES OF INDIAN TERRITORY

On October 3, 1899, a young reporter for the *Denver Times* filed his story from Guthrie, Oklahoma Territory. His assignment—to cover the arrests of Mary Smith and Jessie Findlay, lady outlaws and members of a counterfeiting gang.

Had the *Times* reporter followed up on his story, he might have created another Belle Starr or an early-day Bonnie Parker. The ingredients were all there.

Mary Smith had been a Missouri school teacher when she met a highwayman named Huffman. Leader of an outlaw gang in Indian Territory, he was no Robin Hood, nor was Mary Smith a maiden fair. Mary's attraction for Huffman caused her to quit job, home and friends and ride off with him to the wilds of Oklahoma. But Mary was a fickle young lady and she was soon attracted to another member of the gang. Huffman vowed vengeance on the one who "stole his girl," and his revenge led to the discovery of a wholesale counterfeiting operation.

Two weeks prior to Mary Smith's arrest, her two lovers faced off in a saloon near Caney, Kansas. They reached for their guns and fired simultaneously. When the smoke cleared, both men were down, covered with blood, holding empty six-shooters in their hands. Neither bandit was a deadly shot, however, and both were arrested, patched up, placed in separate cells, and duped by law officers into believing that the other had confessed. Authorities found that the two were members of a counterfeiting gang and both were soured enough on Mary Smith to implicate her as the person who put the bad money into circulation. Mary had been wily enough to distribute more than $100,000 of the privately made money.

The other young lady, Jessie Findlay, was only seventeen, but authorities described her as "one of the most desperate criminals in the country." Jessie was known as an "unerring shot with the revolver, a dashing horsewoman, and absolutely fearless." Her indictment was on charges of smuggling weapons into the county jail to aid gang members in escape, at the cost of the life of the chief of police.

Though still a teenager, Jessie Findlay's bandit life had been long. Four years earlier Bob Christian, leader of the "Christian Gang," had stopped at the Findlay home for dinner. He repaid the kindness by riding off with thirteen-year-old Jessie. Christian taught her to shoot and ride and Jessie became an expert marksman with rifle and revolver.

After the gang members escaped, a posse tracked them, hoping to find Jessie. Alerted to the posse's plan, Jessie disguised herself in cowboy clothes—high-heeled boots, slough hat, and storm coat. But the posse determinedly rode five days, crossing and recrossing their trail. Ultimately they found the girl and by a forced ride of fifty miles through the night, reached a railhead, stopped the train, boarded it with their prisoner, and delivered her to the jail in Oklahoma City.

Within days, Jessie had captured the hearts of her jailers. They reported admiringly that since her imprisonment, Jessie had become a great reader, especially fond of Sir Hall Cains, whose major work then was *Recollections of Rosetti*.

The two young lady counterfeiters provided the *Times* reporter with a great story and another legend of the Old West.

Mary Smith
a lady
of the West

LEARNING THE LESSON OF MURPHY'S LAW

Anything that can go wrong
will go wrong—
                    Murphy's Law

Illinois Governor Henry Horner may have suspected his state's Department of Finance of harboring Murphy. The time was early 1933. Illinois welfare coffers were empty and unemployment set a record. The Illinois senate had just passed an emergency sales tax and on March 22, Horner signed the bill into law, hoping to raise a much needed sixty million dollars.

Just one week later, Murphy's law supervened. A circuit court judge issued an injunction forbidding the collection of sales taxes by the state. Several municipalities circumvented the judge's edict by initiating local sales taxes and issuing tokens to facilitate collection. Litigation continued until finally, on May 10, Horner's state supreme court ruled the tax unconstitutional. The governor's

latest dilemma—how to return more than eight million dollars in pennies already collected.

A new bill was prepared, taking into consideration the court's objections, and passed by the state legislature on June 28. A two percent "occupation" tax, based on the retail price of sale goods and paid by the consumer, overcame the legal objections to a straight sales tax.

Governor Horner was happy. Funds were again available for his welfare projects. On July 1, 1935, the tax rate was raised to three percent. To help collect the proper amount and to protect consumers from overpayments, the state commissioned the striking of ten million round one and one-half-mill aluminum "coins."

Ten days later, Murphy struck again! The state district attorney found that the tokens, similar in size and color to the U.S. ten-cent piece, violated sec. 281, title 18, of the United States Criminal Code. The ten million round tokens were scrapped and Illinois placed another order for thirty million square tokens, with the denomination "mills" removed.

If the Governor thought his problems with state token money were resolved, he overlooked Murphy's Law! The new tokens had been in circulation less than a fortnight, when it was found that counterfeiters were producing them in quantity. Merchants were being offered fake tokens in volume at substantial discounts. Shady store managers were able to pocket for themselves a portion of the tax collected.

Much to the chagrin of state officials, the counterfeiters could not be prosecuted. The legislature had omitted a provision in the statutes to make the copying of the state tokens an offense. Murphy's law ruled again!

Footnote to history:—*Within a year,
Illinois sales tax tokens were out of
circulation except in five-and-dime and
novelty stores. Citizens found the
tokens to be a greater nuisance than
paying the tax in cash. The tokens
were legal until 1945, and (Murphy be
damned) the state offered redemption
until June 30, 1947, but only a few—
real and fake—were ever redeemed.*

THE OL' ONE-EYED CATTS!

Sidney Johnson Catts, Sr., may not
be included on a roster of master
counterfeiters, but he should head the
list of colorful political characters.
Catts, a former Florida governor,
faced an indictment by a Federal
Grand Jury on charges of financing a
counterfeiting ring whose alleged goal
was to put one million dollars of bogus
money into circulation. The year
was 1929.

S.J. Catts, "Ol' One-Eyed Catts,"
as he liked to call himself, was a living
caricature of an old-time politician. He
claimed allegiance to all political
parties and was elected governor of
Florida in 1916 as the Prohibition
candidate. He had sought the Demo-
cratic nomination, but lost it to the
state treasurer. Al Capp fashion, he
stumped the state with a Bible in one
hand and two revolvers strapped
around his waist, winning by a bare
majority of 250 votes!

In 1928, Catts sought the governor-
ship again, this time as a Democrat;
but he campaigned on an anti-Catholic
platform, refusing to support the
party's presidential nominee. Catts
toured the state on behalf of Republi-
can Herbert Hoover. He failed in
the primaries.

S.J.'s life read like an index of
occupations: farmer, merchant,
fertilizer salesman, teacher, preacher,
cowboy, lawyer, politician. Born in
Alabama in 1864, he attended Howard
College and Alabama Polytechnic
Institute. He graduated from law
school and two years later became a
Baptist minister. From the pulpit at
Fort Deposit, Alabama, Catts eyed the
state legislature. Blaming his first
election defeat on his flock, Catts quit
his pulpit dramatically. "I don't expect
to stand here long and see you sitting
like frogs waiting for it to rain. If I
cannot have the support of my congre-
gation, I shall offer my resignation."
It was accepted.

Catts moved to Florida with a wife,
seven children and five-hundred
dollars. Four years later, he was
governor, but not a perfect model of
leadership. When the women's
suffrage amendment passed Congress, Catts chose to ignore it. The
legislature fell into turmoil over his
wholesale dismissal of state employees, replaced with friends. On leaving
office, a Federal Grand Jury indicted
Catts on charges of peonage and
accepting money to buy pardons, but
he was judged not-guilty.

In June 1928, Catts was back in
Florida headlines, charged with
breaking and entering a Defuniak
Springs cafe. The former governor
claimed the restaurant owner owed
him money and planned to leave town,
so he and five other men broke into the
cafe. Sam Satey, the restaurant owner,
admitted the indebtedness—ten
dollars—but claimed that Catts took
the kitchen stove and other items
valued far above the sawbuck due.

Not all Catts' headlining was
political. In partisan speeches he
called himself "Ol One-Eye," having
lost the sight in one eye early in life.
After his gubernatorial stint in Talla-
hasse, he claimed to have gone
completely blind. Newspapers reported a "miracle" cure in 1933, but noted

that his blindness had not kept him from running a successful farm and fertilizer business, nor from filling vacant pulpits whenever a brother of the cloth wanted to rest.

It was the *New York Times* headline of April 10, 1929, that shook the political world of Sidney Johnson Catts, Sr. The headlines read, "Ex-Gov. Catts Is Indicted by Florida Jury On Charge of Financing Counterfeiting Gang." Co-defendants with Catts were Maeto Mir, Armando Dominguez, and Tampa attorney Julian Diaz. Government agents credited the attorney with masterminding and Catts with financing the operation. The former governor allegedly advanced $5,000 to purchase the necessary equipment to print $100 bills, in return for $25,000 in freshly printed notes. Agents claimed the governor had arranged for a New York bank teller to comingle the bogus money with genuine. The counterfeit was said to have been printed in Tampa and distributed in Miami. Easy transactions allowed Government officials to buy the counterfeit at discount—$40 per $1000 lot!

Sidney Catts was as convincing on the stand as he was on the soapbox or behind the pulpit. Insisting that it was a frame-up, Catts' oratory deadlocked the jury. On October 29, 1929, the judge declared a mistrial and "Ol' One-Eyed Catts" was freed.

"Very poorly gotten up," said the government of these dimes

THE BIG SLUG

Today, New York City sports the moniker "Big Apple" but in 1900, one could have called it "The Big Slug." New York, with its large immigrant population, was the counterfeit capital of the United States. Secret Service Chief William P. Hazen concurred, as he recorded the capture of one more gang of *coniakers*, (passers of bad coin, as opposed to *green-goods merchants* who passed bad paper).

This latest apprehension involved a gang far less sophisticated than their aliases implied. James Sullivan, "English Jim;" George West, alias "English Bill;" Timothy Cassidy, who answered to "John Cliff;" and Theodore Stevens, who used his own name and played mintmaster for the gang, were arraigned at noon on Saturday, March 17, 1900, on charges of making and passing counterfeit dimes and half-dollars. All but George West pleaded guilty and were held in the Ludlow Street Jail in lieu of bonds of $5,000 each. West's case was continued until the following Monday.

Chief Hazen informed reporters that the arrest of the gang resulted from shadowing Timothy Cassidy, whose reputation exceeded his counterfeiting skill. Cassidy was first arrested in 1881 on counterfeiting charges and served a six-year term. An 1888 sentence drew one year less. When counterfeit coin complaints were received from the Bowery area, poor Timothy was immediately suspected and shadowed. He was seen meeting the other men, and all were later detected passing slugs. Government agents stalled until they located the money mill in Theodore Stevens' tenement room at 236 East 24th Street on Friday, March 16.

The men under surveillance were

then arrested by Secret Service agents and a raid made on the spurious mint. Searching Stevens' rooms, agents found twelve sets of molds for ten- and fifty-cent pieces, and 200 coins in various steps of manufacture, along with plating apparatus, chemicals and acids. The Government assessed the quality of manufacture as "very poorly gotten up." All coins were dated 1893, the lettering was very bad, and the coin surfaces were streaked and discolored. English Bill and English Jim should have been more conscious of quality. The East 24th Street mint had operated just one week. And, for Timothy Cassidy, St. Patrick's Day, 1900 proved not to be propitious.

TOO NICE A NEIGHBOR-HOOD FOR A MINT

When an employee distinguishes himself in his profession, he often considers going into business for himself. No one at the German Imperial Mint in Berlin seemed surprised, therefore, when Franz Webber said that he wanted to emigrate to America to make money. No one took him literally.

Franz Webber was an expert. In the land of opportunity, he was his own boss and for ten years, operated a very successful home mint. Success could be measured materially by his Academy Street home, then in a very fashionable neighborhood of Astoria, Long Island: and esthetically, by the grudging admiration of his work by the United States Secret Service.

Richard H. Taylor, head of the Secret Service's Manhattan District, mused that Webber's five- and ten-dollar United States Gold Coins were "perfect in appearance, weight and size, but short the prescribed amount of gold!" Webber's half-eagles

contained only three dollars worth of gold, and his eagles were four dollars short.

Wherever Franz went, bad coins were sure to follow. For ten years the Secret Service shadowed the old German, but was unable to secure sufficient evidence for a conviction. There had been a two-year hiatus in Webber's New York residency. Ostensibly, he had journeyed west to work as an assayer for a large mining concern. But, when Webber returned to the New York area, so did short-gold coins. The Secret Service readied its move.

Franz Webber had acquired a partner on his return, Benjamin Lotterer. An undercover agent was assigned to befriend Lotterer, and within a week, the two became pinochle buddies. Soon, the agent was introduced to Webber for three-handed games of pinochle. Gaining the counterfeiters' confidence, the agent was offered an opportunity to make some extra money: a one-third interest in "the gold coin business" if he would help them obtain new equipment and pay a $250 bill due that day on a shipment of metal. The agent agreed and excused himself to go to the bank to make arrangements for the money. Instead, he wired Chief Taylor that the time was right to raid the Astoria home.

Agents John Henry, Otto Klinke and Albert Preusser were assigned to the stakeout. Sunday at precisely 10 a.m., December 11, 1910, as church bells

A short-weight five-dollar gold piece

pealed, the agents struck. Seized was a cartload of molds, steel bowls, alloy mixers and the gold the agent had underwritten for them.

Parishioners of the Protestant Episcopal Church of the Redeemer stopped to watch agents, with pistols drawn, race across the spacious grounds of the Academy Street house. The horse-drawn paddy wagon pulled up and the handcuffed Franz Webber and Benjamin Lotterer were trotted off to the Adams Street Station in Brooklyn. The entire raid took little more than ten minutes and brought an end to the ten-year career of the former German mint employee who came to America "to make money."

A MARRIAGE CERTIFICATE TELLS ALL

Turn-of-the-century apartments along New York's Lower East Side were sparsely furnished, but a place of honor was usually reserved for the tenant's framed marriage certificate. The apartment at 511 East Eleventh Street was no exception, although David Friedman would always regret displaying his certificate so prominently on the wall.

The apartment resembled more a miser's treasure house than a place to live. In the oven, on top of shelves in the closets, in and under the beds, were hoards of dimes and quarters— hundreds of them—all Barber dimes, all Morgan quarters, all the same date, and all spurious. The apartment harbored a fully equipped private mint, capable of turning out hundreds of good copies of United States coins daily.

For several months in 1908, the Washington office of the Secret Service had been receiving complaints about the large number of counterfeit dimes and quarters then circulating in the eastern part of the country. Most of the reports came from areas around New York City and Newark, New Jersey.

Several operatives were assigned to this case, including agents Richard Jarvese and Daniel Callahan. They were soon on the trail of two men believed to be runners for the private mint. Jarvese and Callahan finally arrested the pair in Newark as they were about to board a New York train. Several dollars worth of spurious dimes and quarters were found, but for several hours the two refused to talk, or even identify themselves.

Pressured, in the days before prisoners' rights were paramount, the pair "weakened" and gave their names as Morris Ebstein and Alexander Edelman. They said they obtained their bogus change at 511 East Eleventh.

Accompanied by two Newark detectives, the agents went to New York and were joined by two police officers. The posse then headed for the Lower East Side, armed with a fire axe, forced entry into the suspect apartment, but found it unoccupied. A search uncovered suspect coins in every imaginable hiding place. After a thorough search, the agents turned off the lights and waited for the tenants to return. The wait was in vain. Questioning neighbors produced no results; no one knew the tenants. But David Friedman's proud display of his marriage certificate provided all the information the agents needed.

Base metal quarter

ALL IN THE FAMILY

The Mannarano family had fallen on hard times. Three generations shared a cramped Rivington Street flat in a crowded tenement district of New York City. They survived by augmenting their monthly home-relief income with family enterprise.

Despite the adversity, the family stayed together—father Lorenzo, wife Nancy, son Paul, his wife Mary and grandchildren. Now, on March 17, 1940, all four adults were being bound over to the Grand Jury to face charges of counterfeiting.

Counterfeiting was a Mannarano family tradition. Lorenzo, the family patriarch, had already served one three-year sentence for practicing his art in 1926. Charles was currently serving a term for counterfeiting at Lewisburg Penitentiary.

Commissioner Isaac Platt set Lorenzo's bail at $10,000 (genuine money), but released Mary, his daughter-in-law, on her own recognizance because she had a small child. The two remaining family members were held in lieu of $1,000 each.

At the time of the Secret Service raid on their flat, Mannarano home products were beginning to enjoy a boom. Increased productivity necessitated an additional sales force. Representing the city proper was Albert Caprano; Brooklyn was covered by Louis Vero, both of whom faced Commissioner Platt.

Secret Service agents grudgingly admitted that the Mannarano half-dollars, quarters, and dimes were of "excellent" quality. Over $500 in face was discovered in their flat, with the paraphernalia necessary to cast their money.

MONEY TO BUY A PARDON

Lee Jayer and Joseph Vail had much in common. Both cellmates were serving long sentences in the Missouri State Penitentiary at Jefferson City. Incarceration meant idle hours, and Jayer and Vail speculated on what they would do if they had a little money.

Their plot was a tribute to the ingenuity of confined men and it earned them a governor's pardon. Under the very noses of inquisitive guards, Jayer and Vail built a fully equipped counterfeiting plant. The pair kept production limited and for a while produced a good imitation of real money. Their quarters and half-dollars fooled the commissary trustee, but their volume eventually raised enough suspicion to warrant a cell search.

Missouri Governor Hadley found, to his chagrin, that prosecution on counterfeiting charges would have to wait until Jayer and Vail completed their current terms. Rather than wait, the governor pardoned the men from their current sentence. In October 1910, Jayer and Vail were released—to face counterfeiting charges. Still, their fake quarters and half-dollars were good enough to have bought a clean slate on prior convictions!

Counterfeit Washington quarter

Quarters that bought a pardon

NOT QUITE WHAT THE DOCTOR ORDERED

For hypochondriacs, physicians generally have an understanding attitude, a knowing smile, a ready placebo, and a bill to match the patient's social standing. Carmela Briganti fit this profile, but took it one step further—she made it pay.

It was mid-1941, still months away from America's entry into World War II. Doctors still made house calls and the cost of office visits ranged from $3 to $5. New York City physicians sympathized with Miss Briganti, often giving her a sample prescription or sugar pill, and change for the five-, ten-, or twenty-dollar bill she usually tendered.

The change was genuine, but Carmela's money was as counterfeit as her illnesses. Miss Briganti was the passer of bogus money for a ring Federal agents described as "one of the few sizable counterfeiting rings remaining since the Treasury Department began its intensive campaign against fake money passers several years ago."

On November 25, 1941, a Federal Grand Jury investigation culminated in the arrest of eight men and one woman—Carmela Briganti—on charges of illegal manufacture, possession and distribution of counterfeit money. In addition to exchanging bogus money for nostrums and genuine change from doctors, Carmela had a second, equally unique caper. She developed a literal have-your-cake-and-eat-it-too routine. Victims of this scam were bakers exchanging good labor for bad paper. Carmela would doe-eye a susceptible baker and order a birthday cake.

"Please put 'To Mother' on it," she'd ask. For such a pretty young girl, few old dough-rollers could resist adding an extra decoration or two. For their pains, they would receive a bouncing bill. The routine was repeated enough for Carmela to have felt like Marie Antoinette, had she known her history.

Judge Henry Goddard sentenced the men to terms ranging from eighteen months to two years. But, when it came to Carmela, Judge Goddard ruled from the heart, joining many doctors and bakers who had been her victims. Carmela scored again. Although she had passed most of the funny money made by the gang, the judge reasoned that since she received "such a tiny portion" of the proceeds, a suspended sentence was more than adequate to rebalance the scales of justice.

TWENTY-FIVE CENTS BUYS A FREE TRIP!

Boxed by rows along the sidewalk in front of Fred Steeneck's store at 50 Bank Street in Greenwich Village are the shiniest and firmest apples from Upstate New York, grapes from New England Arbors, oranges and grapefruit from Florida, berries of all sorts from Jersey farms, plums from the South. Good business practice demands keeping one eye fixed on the fruit in front; this is a neighborhood where five-finger discounts are a way of life. Steeneck knows his customers, if not by name, at least by habits and preferences.

Michael Limatalo lives nearby, at 29 Cornelia Street, with his wife and two stepdaughters—Frances Carro, 18, and Ray Carro, 19. They are regular customers, but lately have limited their purchases to five cents at a time. They always pay in quarters, sometimes coins of the Liberty Standing design, occasionally with the newer Washington head composition. Steeneck fails to keep the same sharp eye on his cash box as he does his fruit boxes and his money spoils faster than his fruit. At day's end, he has more bad quarters than bad apples.

On a lead furnished by Steeneck, Secret Service agents and detectives from the Charles Street Station stake out the fruit stand. Limatalo and his stepdaughters are arrested after passing five homemade coins to Steeneck in return for fruit munchies during the day.

In searching the Limatalo home, they find nine molds for casting quarters. They also discover that Limatalo entered the United States by jumping ship in 1927. His private minting operations lead authorities to suggest that the Bureau of Immigration invest in a one-way steamship ticket to Italy, noting that lead slugs do not buy first-class accommodations.

A large number of counterfeit quarters circulated in the summer of 1940

IT'S THE QUALITY THAT COUNTS

Augustus Saint Gaudens had completed work on his new ten-dollar coin for the United States Treasury. Eighteen months of study and experimentation went into various designs before he settled on a profile of Victory, an adaptation of one of his figures from the General Sherman monument in New York's Central Park. Victory was capped with an Indian bonnet at the suggestion of President Theodore Roosevelt. Saint Gaudens' creation initiated a new era in American coin design.

Lee Young studied Saint Gaudens' masterpiece with the intensity of an art student tracing the brush strokes of the master, but Young's creativity in coinage art was limited to copying. From his isolated tropical island home, the young Oriental artist reasoned that a good living could be earned copying the work of Augustus Saint Gaudens. Young was quite confident that the average person would not be able to detect any differences in their work; his success as a counterfeiter depended on this.

Saint Gaudens' ten-dollar gold eagle was too new for many to be familiar with the design, but this proved to be Young's downfall—his coins were examined too carefully! A visit to Young's remote Maui hut in the Hawaiian Islands, by U.S. District Attorney Breckons and Marshall Hendry, uncovered a completely outfitted counterfeiting plant. In his mint, Young had produced "almost" excellent copies of Augustus Saint Gaudens' new ten-dollar gold pieces. Government assay revealed Young's reward to be in the quality of the work and not in seigniorage. His gold content approximated that of the government issues!

THE TENTH TERM OF JOHN MURRAY

John Murray nickeled and dimed his way to infamy. His lifetime obsession with making his own five- and ten-cent pieces earned him a minimum of ten prison terms and editorial mention in the October 11, 1918, edition of the *New York Times*.

John Murray would never rank among the clever or talented counterfeiters of the world, but perhaps one of the most persevering. Murray's work was crude, clumsy and failed to improve with experience. He was a loser, and the *Times'* editorial writer took pity on him:

"Something of that mystery of human destiny that stares at us from the eyes of the maniac or the idiot invites strange questionings in such a case as that of John Murray of Chicago, 68 years of age, just sent to Leavenworth Prison to serve his tenth term for the counterfeiting of nickels and dimes. What is experience worth, and who shall make the crooked straight?

"Murray began going to prison in 1882. The chief pay he has got from his passion for making bad five- and ten-cent pieces is a sum of jail sentences amounting to thirty-nine years and one-half. The moderation of his ambition has not helped him. One scrutinizes a nickel and a dime less carefully than a five- or ten-dollar bill, but, evidently, Murray is a bad artist. His craftsmanship is defective. He cannot hit even the small deer he shoots at. He is always caught. As soon as he gets out of the "clink" he goes back to his old profession, practices it with his wonted clumsiness, is caught again.

"Certain beautiful copy-book expressions about value of industry and perseverance and devotion to a single aim leer sarcastically from the record of John Murray. So does the virtuous commonplace about 'weakness of the will.' John Murray was not the victim of 'divided aims.' He had but one aim, and stuck to it, and will stick to it, no doubt if he survives his tenth term. He, too, 'saw life steadily and saw it whole,' saw it as a place where you make bad nickels and bad dimes."

October 11, 1918
New York Times

Life is a place to make bad dimes

MADE IN MEXICO

The U.S. Department of Commerce and the State Department have always encouraged intercourse with Mexico. Quality products manufactured south of the border and exported to the Untied States earn much needed foreign revenue for Mexico and give their citizens the capital to buy American goods. Both countries benefit from a mutual trade. Jose Frias made a product that met with instant acceptance, which concerned (or rather *alarmed*) Chief John E. Wilkie of the Secret Service Division of the Treasury Department.

The Government of Porfirio Diaz had exploited the Indians and the Mestizos, but had not discouraged free enterprise. Jose Frias answered the call by establishing a private mint for the conversion of Mexican pesos to Yankee dollars. Frias' enterprise was so successful that he had difficulty meeting demand. Specimens of his Mexican-made dollars circulated as far north as New York City. Despite its good neighbor policy, the American government was not appreciative of cheap foreign competition.

Jose Frias' method of manufacture was out of the ordinary. He took Mexican one-peso coins, a little heavier than American silver dollars, trimmed them to weight, and over-struck Morgan's Liberty head design on them. Since the Mexican pesos traded at two to the dollar, Frias was doubling his investment! Since Frias' coins were struck on good silver, the ring of the money was proper when put to an auditory test.

So concerned was the Secret Service that the U.S. sent a representative to Mexico to ask for Diaz' help, but as Frias was making only U.S. coins, the Mexican government at first declined help. Ultimately, with prodding, Mexican authorities reversed them-selves, remembering a law that prohibited the unauthorized conver-sion of Mexican money into that of another country. Jose Frias was arrested and the Mexican-made American silver dollar trade came to an end.

ANOTHER MINT IN DENVER!

When the U.S. Government pur-chased the minting plant of Clark, Gruber & Company in 1863, Denver-ites expected minting operations to continue and new coins to bear the ''D'' mintmark. But ''D'' stood for disappointment. Although it was officially called a mint, the Treasury facility in Denver served only as an assay office until 1906.

Government records show, how-ever, that many five-, ten-, and twenty-dollar gold pieces were made in Denver prior to 1906. Although not officially coined or bearing the Denver mintmark, the coins were of U.S. design and the makers allegedly had the backing of influential Colorado citizens. Regardless of manufacture date, the coins (with the exception of the twenty-dollar gold pieces) bore the date 1880. The double eagles were dated 1886.

In mid-March, 1899, despite the ''influential backing,'' United States marshalls swooped down on the unofficial mint in Denver. W.H. Elliott and Arthur States were arrested and jailed in Pueblo, Colorado, away from their ''influential'' friends. Officers complained that the two were abusive in their language and had to be handcuffed to the seats in their cells.

Mexican-made U.S. silver dollars were struck over Mexican pesos

Around-the-clock surveillance was necessary during their Pueblo stay.

Wanted for six years, Elliott was described as "one of the smoothest men in the business in the United States." He had developed a special composition for the manufacture of his coins; when the castings were gold plated, they had the "ring" of genuine currency. Samples were sent to Washington for analysis.

The master counterfeiter had a legitimate occupation, too. He traveled the country selling hand-colored photographs, distributing his spurious products at the same time. But Elliott's biggest caper was in the making at the time of his arrest. He and States were stockpiling their product, preparing for a visit to the gold mining towns of Colorado. Their plan was to sell their coin to gold miners.

As for their "influential" backers, they were either too important or non-existent to be implicated.

A DAY IN THE LIFE OF A GRAND JUROR

In 1900, Pueblo was the second largest city in Colorado. Home of the huge Colorado Fuel and Iron Works, the city was called the Pittsburgh of the West. Pueblo was also the location for the spring term of the Federal Grand Jury. A number of citizens were summoned, and it appeared to many that Colorado was populated with people more interested in making their own money than earning an honest dollar.

On April 20, 1900, a number of indictments were handed down against counterfeiters. Some cases seemed ludicrous, others were tragicomical:

The Unlucky Trio

James L. Vincent, his brother Lee, and Andrew Jackson McElroy, were Missouri farmers who found their fortunes as poor as the soil they worked. Pooling their meager resources, they moved to Colorado and purchased a piece of equipment seldom found on a farm—a plating battery costing twenty-five dollars, as well as gallons of gold, silver and copper solutions, and a quantity of plaster of Paris. The trio told acquaintances that they were going into the gold ring plating business, and actually made one ring!

Along with the ring, the Vincents and McElroy made a number of plaster of Paris molds of a communal ten-dollar gold piece. They selected the casts with the fewest imperfections and gold plated them. Discretion prevented them from cashing their coins locally, so they selected a mining town a day's journey away. Ouray, Colorado, was a town so rich in gold, they assumed no one would examine a paltry gold eagle too closely, but dame fortune was not with the counterfeiters.

Lee Vincent and Andrew McElroy tried to pass their first coin on former Ouray sheriff and past town marshall of Telluride, Colorado. He refused their coin. Meanwhile, James Vincent was casing taverns, his face pressed so hard against one window that his nose was flattened. Bartender Thomas Sloane suspected a hold-up and reached for his revolver. Vincent entered the bar, ordered a beer, and turned his back to Sloan to drink it. Sloan, a former police officer had so anticipated a hold-up, that he scarcely glanced at the ten-dollar gold eagle placed on the counter. He gave Vincent the proper change and carefully watched the man. Not until

Vincent left, as the coin "clunked" into his cash drawer, did Sloan realize that he had been the victim of a different kind of crime.

Sloan summoned police officers, they compared experiences and went looking for the trio. By the time of the April Grand Jury, Lee Vincent and Andrew Jackson McElroy were already serving their sentences at the state penitentiary at Canon City, Colorado. James Vincent was soon to be reunited with his partners.

All For The Promise of a Slot Machine

The next case to be heard by the Grand Jury was that of John Eshelman and Carl Schinick, indicted for counterfeiting five-cent pieces. The pair had no intention of trying to pass their money in commerce; they simply wanted to strike it rich in slot machine jackpots and their coins were made solely for this purpose. They were caught pursuing their dream in Aspen, Colorado. Schinick was busy feeding the nickel slots, Eshelman waiting his turn, when the city marshall, N.A. Likens, chanced by.

When asked by a juror why they bothered to counterfeit genuine nickels when plain, blank slugs would have sufficed, the pair seemed stunned. It had never occurred to them! Instead of being charged with the misdemeanor of slugging a slot machine, Eshelman and Schinick faced a Federal offense.

Counterfeit ten-dollar gold eagle

A Well Equipped Pantry

At the turn of the century, almost every household had a jar or bowl for stashing away a few dollars for a rainy day. In the pantry at 2236 Curtis Street in Denver, there were more than just coins; there were the molds used to make them, too.

The Grand Jury, on April 20, 1900, returned an indictment against Mattie Coffman for having in her possession plaster matrices used for casting silver dollars. Police found a complete counterfeiting outfit in the lady's pantry. In the cellar, metal spatterings were "all over the floor." Ms. Coffman had ignored her housekeeping to devote time to her money making project. Her trial was scheduled for the May term of the United States Court at Denver.

SO WHAT'S A PLUGGED NICKEL?

To the odds-makers at the 1980 Kentucky Derby, Plugged Nickle (sic) was a three-to-one pre-race favorite. To coin collectors, not inclined to gamble, it was worth a two dollar bet. Although Plugged Nickle led, going into the quarter-mile, he jammed in the slot and finished out of the money(!) And to think that Plugged Nickle was the offspring of Toll Booth, sired by Key to the Mint. Honest!

Numismatically, what is a "plugged nickel"? It is not listed in the *Dictionary of Numismatic Terms*, or the *Oxford Dictionary on the Origin of Words*. A line in the *American Thesaurus of Slang* defines it as something worthless or insignificant. But plugged nickels have a place in numismatic history, and if you lived in the 1930s you may have seen one.

Pre-World War II clubs, bars and

Hollow in the center to make them lighter than the circulating five-cent piece, these tokens were often used, with the aid of a lead plug, to cheat

vendors and the telephone company. The practice gave us the term "plugged nickel", meaning worthless or insignificant

candy shops had vending machines that paid off in free games. Instead of automatically registering the free games, the machines paid off in tokens, which theoretically went back into the machines for more games. But more often then not, the tokens bought gum, mints, cigarettes or even cash.

In order to comply with a U.S. code which prohibited the distribution of any tokens, slugs or discs similar in size and shape to any lawful coin of the United States, manufacturers produced tokens with large holes in the center. This made the token lighter and supposedly different in shape from the five-cent piece. But a simple lead plug, surreptitiously added later, brought the token up to a weight sufficient to trip the coin mechanism of juke boxes, vending machines and pay phones—enough to violate the law and relegate the holed token, the plugged nickel of yesteryear—to the junk box of today's coin dealer, nostalgia from the 1930s.

THE COUNTERFEIT THAT SHATTERS DREAMS

"This coin has been in our family for generations."

"Going through the ruins of an old mining town, I found this coin with my metal detector."

"I have a gold piece that was willed to me by my grandfather."

"I was plowing a field for spring planting and found this unusual $20 gold piece. A local dealer offered me a thousand dollars for it, but I know it's more valuable than that."

If prizes were given for fiction to "finders" of Blake & Company twenty-dollar gold pieces, I would be hard pressed to determine the most original, since some guidebooks list the piece as "priceless," and there is some speculation among experts as to whether the piece really existed. There was, indeed, a Blake & Company, assayers in California during the gold rush. The firm was originally known as Blake & Agnell, and operated a gold smelting and assaying plant at 52 J Street in Sacramento in 1855. Later in the year,

Gorham Blake and W.R. Waters formed a partnership. Blake & Company opened for business on December 29, 1855, an important date to remember. The firm continued under that name until 1859 when Blake retired and it became Waters & Company.

The twenty-dollar assay pieces of so much controversy first became known in the mid-1950s. In 1960 these were listed in the *Guidebook of United States Coins*, the "red book," or Bible of the hobby. Only two were known, probably made in the closing days of 1855. By 1966 the controversy reached the point that the listing and photographs were dropped from the book and a single line listed it as a piece under study.

The company did strike some trial pieces dated 1856, but these bore the head of Liberty on the obverse and an eagle, similar to the U.S. twenty-dollar gold piece, on the reverse. These pieces likely reflected the final effort by private firms in California to issue gold coins. In 1856 the operations of the U.S. Mint in San Francisco were extremely limited and other private assay firms had ceased to make coins. The scarcity caused talk of resuming the private issues and this is likely the reason behind Blake & Company patterns.

But the 1856 pattern is not the one people are finding. The piece causing the problems is dated 1855. Since the company was not even founded until December 29 of that year, there is serious doubt that dies were prepared in advance or were made in the two remaining days of the year.

Where are all these pieces coming from? Replicas have been made of many private issues, but why so many Blake & Company?

In 1972, Chrysler-Plymouth Corporation as a promotion offered an "Old West Coin Collection" of twelve private issue gold coins for $7.75. These were all cast replicas with a thin gold wash. The Blake & Company twenty-dollar gold piece dated 1855 was not in the set! This piece was given free to everyone who visited the Chrysler-Plymouth showrooms to test drive the new Gold Duster! Few apparently purchased the set of twelve, but not so with the free token offer.

Not all owners have fabricated a story on how they obtained the piece; many have been duped into buying a worthless imitation. Young collectors may have been given tokens by those who did test drive a Gold Duster but neglected to relate its origin. Fortunately, we now have a law to protect against such abuses. The Hobby Protection Act requires the date of manufacture to be placed on restrikes and replicas or the word COPY, but this cannot be made retroactive to pieces made before 1975.

Cast replicas of the Blake & Company twenty-dollar gold piece abound

UNCOMMON TALES OF COMMON COUNTERFEITERS -- Part III

THE MONEY MACHINES OF COUNT LUSTIG

If the *King of Con* is ever crowned the title must go to Victor Lustig. Actually, Lustig had more modest aspirations—he preferred *Count*. His claim to underworld royalty stemmed from his grand coup—selling the Eiffel Tower not once, but twice. The subjects of his wiles were not simple tourists—he pulled the grand con on some leading tradesmen of Paris.

Victor Lustig was a man of ritual. Like other Parisian gentlemen, he generally spent an hour daily at a favorite sidewalk cafe on one of the boulevards near his hotel, enjoying a cup of *cafe noir* and perusing the afternoon paper. It was Paris in the Spring, and somewhere in the paper of May 8, 1925 was a small filler story concerning the Eiffel Tower. Lustig turned to look at the tower dominating the city skyline and then turned back to this story.

Inspiration struck, and he was on his way to creating one of the great scams of the century. The afternoon edition of the paper reported that the Eiffel Tower was in dire need of work and might be torn down to save money.

To perpetrate his scheme, Lustig had to reproduce the letterhead of The Ministry of Posts and Telegraphs, for it was under their jurisdiction that the tower fell. Next he researched the height and weight of the Eiffel Tower, the number and structure of main girders, the tonnage of the interlaced ironwork, the number of rivets— everything a scrap metal dealer might require. Five letters of invitation on the forged stationery were hand delivered to selected scrap metal dealers, inviting each to a meeting so confidential that it could not be conducted at the Ministry chambers.

When they assembled in Lustig's hotel suite, the dealers were sworn to secrecy and told that the government was going to dismantle the tower. They had been invited to bid on the scrapping of the tower. Confidentiality was paramount; the sale must be completed before the public could be told—*fait accompli!*

As Lustig watched the dealers, one appeared more gullible than the others. Adding insult to injury, the Count hinted that he was an underpaid government employee, not above a perk or two. To insure that his bid would be accepted, the dealer slipped him a bribe—a check made out in Lustig's name to insure Ministry secrecy. Before the day was over, Lustig had cashed the $50,000 check and was on a train for Vienna.

Perhaps the dealer realized he had been conned and, in embarrassment, never filed a complaint. Several months later Lustig returned to pull his trick again. This time he netted $75,000 and his victim was far from silent. Lustig fled to the U.S.-America was ripe for a different con.

Greed and a get-rich-quick ethic were Lustig's partners in crime. His money box trick was known as a "short con" in the world of hucksterism and Lustig baited merchants, tradesmen, gamblers, even a Texas sheriff and a California banker. The money box was a simple affair: a few gears, fewer cranks, a place to put ink and chemicals, a false bottom, and a slot for emerging notes that looked "as good as genuine". In theory, a genuine note and a blank piece of paper were inserted into the machine, and the image of the genuine "chemically" transferred to the blank piece of paper, leaving the original note and a "perfect" copy.

Lustig didn't bother with those unable to "think big." He never sold machines for less than $4,000 and a California banker paid $100,000 for his model! Lustig's demonstrations were convincing. Realizing that some of his rubes might be suspicious, he insured that the serial numbers of his "reproductions" were the same as those on his masters by alternating one set of serial numbers beforehand.

Treasury agents were chagrined. They could not arrest Lustig because his box "produced" genuine money, not counterfeit. The Government never thought to charge him with altering currency with intent to defraud!

Lustig subsequently sold one of his machines to a Texas sheriff who paid for it with county funds. The sheriff captured the conning Count, but then let Lustig talk his way out of it. He told the sheriff that he had used the money from the box to buy a set of perfect printing plates for U.S. currency and would make the sheriff an equal partner if he could raise $65,000 to buy a printing press to make the notes. County funds were short once again.

The story Lustig told the sheriff inspired him to print real counterfeit. From 1930 to 1935, he was very successful. Before he was apprehended on September 19, 1935, he had peddled two and one-half million dollars in "queer."

Lustig managed one escape from jail—although freedom was brief—by copying on old movie stunt—tying bedsheets together and climbing out a window. Passersby watched the daytime escape, one commenting, "what an unusual way to wash windows!" The Count was apprehended and served the remainder of his life in prison. Before he died at Leavenworth in 1947, fellow inmates, in perverted pride, bestowed on Lustig the title "King of Con."

A GYPSY RHAPSODY

Louis Veronach was a salesman with a purpose, "drive" in Dale Carnegie terminology. If Veronach had to marry has client's daughter to clinch a sale, so be it, even if his own wife had to act as bridesmaid.

Louis Veronach (also known as Samuel Gersey, Louis Kroll, or George Batoni) was a gypsy: tall, brown eyed, handsome, and had been called "a talented" violinist. What lonely heart could resist such charms?

The subject of Veronach's latest sales pitch was the owner of a Pittsburgh delicatessen. The object was to sell him a money machine: a device about the size of a carpenter's toolbox, a machine Veronach guaranteed to turn out perfectly counterfeit banknotes, by simply feeding plain bond paper into the machine. To show his sincerity, Veronach wooed, then married, the delicatessen owner's daughter. Bigamy was incidental, as the paper said, for the sake of a sale.

Gypsy Violinist is Charged With Clearing $100,000 Through Old Fraud

---

BIGAMY ONLY AN INCIDENT

Police Declare He Wed Girl to Impress Wealthy Father, with First Wife as Bridesmaid

The extra marital step was not necessary to make the sale. He had recently closed sales on more than $100,000 worth of money machines— in 1919 when annual wages averaged less than $2,000 per year!

Police reported Veronach to be part of a gang of ten men engaged in promoting the money machine caper. At the time of Veronach's arrest, most of the gang were cellmates at Sing Sing, including Veronach's real father-in-law.

How did the newest Mrs. Veronach take the news? Not her Louis! She wrangled father into digging deeper into his savings to hire a lawyer for Louis and he sought her Lothario's release through a writ of *habeas corpus*. Alas—she was as unsuccessful with the law as she was with love.

THE STORY OF THE COUNTERFEIT PENNIES

The last official mint in Boston ceased production in the late eighteenth century after making half-cent and large cent pieces for commonwealth circulation. Officials a century later were surprised therefore, when they raided a machine shop and found a completely equipped mint, operated by men with high hopes and low expectations. Their sole product was reproductions of one-cent pieces of the United States.

Secret Service records say two out of every 100 one-cent pieces of 1884 and 1893 are counterfeit. Production averaged more than 5,000 coins a week for at least five years, making one and one-quarter million of the seventy million one-cent pieces spurious. Officials termed them "of excellent workmanship, and with the little attention given to pennies by the average citizen not one in a thousand would notice anything wrong."

The Boston "mint" pennies had a peculiar hue, said experts, "as though they had been immersed in some acid to give them the appearance of age." A close inspection showed that the edges were slightly uneven.

The tale resembled a dime novel— poor little girl duped into being a runner for a band of nefarious counterfeiters; a meticulous Secret Service chief; a sharp-eyed Government agent of Chinese ancestry; an unsympathetic judge; set in the steamy hand laundries of New York's Chinatown.

The story broke on Sunday morning, February 10, 1901. Reporters with sentimental bents helped many readers shed tears before church. Others were a little skeptical: "Counterfeiting copper cents would hardly seem to offer profit sufficiently commensurate with the risk to engage a gang of expert coiners."

The making of spurious cents was no moonlighting operation. It was full time, complete with a network of distributors and passers. Samples were found throughout the country, particularly in the northeast corridor.

Of the Indian head cents of 1884 and 1893, two out of every hundred were probably counterfeit

Little Fanny Lenhart, a thirteen-year old denizen of the streets of New York, brought the operation to light unintentionally. On Friday morning, February 1, Dr. Jin Fuey Moy was paying an official visit to the laundry of Hung Lee at 4 Rivington Street in lower Manhattan. As Dr. Moy and Charley Kee, another Government agent, discussed business with the laundryman, a little girl entered the laundry, wrapped in rags on the bitter cold, mid-winter morning. From under her shawl she took a roll of pennies, tightly wrapped in brown paper and sealed, and offered them to the proprietor. The laundry man broke open the roll, counted and added the coins to his cash box while Dr. Moy watched. All had a peculiar hue and the same date—1893.

When Dr. Moy suggested that something was wrong, Fanny became quite agitated, insisting that the amount was correct. Charley Kee was sent to find a policeman, and Fanny admitted she had received the coins from a man waiting for her on Allen Street who had promised her a few pennies for changing his coin. The officials let her go, but followed her from a distance. When Fanny's confederate failed to show, officers brought her to the Essex Market Police Court and summoned a Secret Service agent to take charge of the case. Fanny Lenhart was secretly arrested, arraigned before a city magistrate, and later before a United States commissioner. She was subsequently released but kept under constant surveillance. On February 9, Fanny was rearrested and jailed. This time her arraignment was public and she was represented by counsel. A number of witnesses were called, including Lee Sing of 142 Chrystie Street, who testified that he had been buying pennies from Fanny in lots of fifty or a hundred for almost a year. After other similar testimony, Little Fanny was ordered held in lieu of $1,5000 bail and committed to the care of the Gerry Society.

Fanny Lenhart was one of the youngest prisoners ever arrested for passing counterfeit money. Secret Service agents visited the girl's home, a squalid two-room apartment in a tenement at 167 Suffolk Street. They found only a few spurious pennies mixed with a few real ones—Fanny's employers paid her with their own brand of coin.

Officials found no reason to implicate the little girl's parents, but they did pursue the clandestine operations of the penny makers. At the time, more than five thousand spurious cents a week were being turned in to the sub-treasury on Wall Street and destroyed. How many were escaping detection, no government agent could guess.

For the next eight months, Treasury agents continued their investigation. Then on October 28, 1901, simultaneous raids in a number of eastern cities brought operations to an end. M. Weiner was arrested in Boston on charges of making the coins. Israel Usher, also of Boston, was charged with passing them. Brooklyn jeweler M. Levine, was charged with having bought the steel used in making the dies. Henry Lerner and his daughter Rosa were arrested in Baltimore. In Boston officials found a complete plant including a press and material for making the coins.

When asked if the profit justified the risk, a Secret Service spokesman replied, "Counterfeiting cents is one of the most profitable, as well as one of the safest branches of nefarious coining. One pound of copper at eighteen cents stamps out $1.30 in pennies."

THE BITTER OF SWEET REVENGE

From 1894 through 1896, and again in 1909, hundreds of thousands of Armenians living in Turkey were killed or exiled. Most of those fortunate enough to escape to the U.S. settled in three metropolitan areas: New York, Providence, Rhode Island, and Worcester, Massachusetts.

At first they headed for the "Little Armenias" in the overcrowded slum sections of these cities where they took temporary jobs, but many Armenians shared a desire to become businessmen themselves. They also shared a hatred of the Turks, and although free of domination by them, revenge was fresh in their minds. One resourceful new citizen found a way to combine free enterprise with revenge.

Kirkor Dederian was one who immigrated to Providence, the jewelry city. In an old industrial area, Dederian leased most of the top floor of an old building for his new business, the Eagle Stamping Company. Dederian assembled a forge, milling machines, rolling mills, a stamping press, and annealing equipment—all that was needed to operate a small, modern and efficient mint.

Kirkor Dederian Americanized his name to K. Gregory. His burning hatred of the Turks still rampant, he sought revenge. In addition to badges, nameplates and jewelry findings, Dederian added the 100-piastre Turkish gold coins of Abdul Hamid II "The Damned" to his production.

Late in the afternoon of February 26, 1916, a team of Federal agents raided Dederian's plant to find him at his workbench touching up the Turkish gold pieces of his own manufacture. As the officers moved in, Dederian hurled several of the coins into a pile of debris.

Dederian had come to the agency's attention six weeks earlier when several bogus Turkish gold coins appeared in the shop of a Providence coin dealer. Secret Service chief W.J. Flynn ordered Dederian's plant placed under surveillance. With the jailing of Dederian, Flynn noted that he had one of the most complete counterfeiting plants he had ever viewed. The coins were struck, not cast, and "beautifully finished!"

Abdul Hamid II was never aware of Dederian's attempted revenge. The Turkish sultan, persecutor of the Armenian people, was himself deposed in 1909. Tragically, the attempted genocide of the Armenians by the Turks did not end with Abdul Hamid, The Damned.

THE ENRICHED DIMES OF SPAIN

In the rush for uranium during the post-war dawn of the nuclear age, there was one who gave thought to prospecting—not uranium itself, but the related publicity. His name is lost to history: a shame, too, for he found a way to turn aluminum centimos into silvered pesetas, and profit handsomely. His formula blended greed with ignorance. He attempted to corner the market on 1945 dated, aluminum ten-centimos coins of Spain. It was an awesome task, considering that 250 million were made (ten for each man, woman, and child in the country). If he could not corner the entire issue, then he would garner all that circulated in Catalonia, or at least in Barcelona. The investment would be minimal—the face value of the coin was far less than one American cent.

The wily promoter stockpiled enough 1945 ten-centimos coins to create a scarcity in the northeastern part of the country. Now he had to create a demand—not by coin collectors, for there were far too few in impoverished Spain in 1946—but among the peasants, for here were great numbers.

The modern charlatan simply started a rumor that Spain's 1945 ten-centimos were made on metal sufficiently rich in uranium to power all the atomic energy needs of the country. The gullible found few of the 1945 coins in circulation, but there was one source, a street vendor who created a mini-gold rush, selling ten-centimos coins for five pesetas each, a modest mark-up of 5,000 percent! When the facts became known, the story-teller-cum-coin-dealer skipped town, taking with him his profits and the secret of his name.

THE JIG-SAW CURRENCY

It was 1927; high living, fast cars, and art deco were the order of the day. In keeping with the time, France replaced the 1000-franc note that had served it well since 1889, with a beautifully designed, multi-colored note of predominant blue and ochre. There were heads of Ceres, the Roman goddess of grain, and Mercury, Roman god of commerce, with two small cherubic angels forming part of the border. This single 1000-franc note represented a sizable fortune for ex-printer Raymond Marty—about $200 or ten weeks wages.

Marty fantasized handing one of the bills to a waiter as he enjoyed *petit dejeuner* at a sidewalk restaurant in La Bastide-Saint Pierre. He mentally counted the pile of change, all genuine.

Marty's thoughts turned to counterfeiting the handsome 1000-franc notes,

but he lacked the engraving skills necessary to duplicate the intricate designs. Why not commission a legitimate engraving company to duplicate the note? The design was so new that it might not be recognized, at least not in another country. Marty designed a number of fantasy pieces, each using a particular feature of the legitimate bill. The companies were to make the engraving plates only; Marty would do his own printing.

When he placed his orders, one firm in Brussels was immediately suspicious. The firm notified Belgian police who were on hand to greet Marty when he picked up his order. The police told Marty that part of the design seemed similar to the new 1000-franc notes of France. Laughed Marty, "You have vivid imaginations. Why not compare the designs?" The gendarmes consented, but no one had a genuine 1000-franc note. The police left to find a note for comparison and Marty left, too!

Belgian authorities notified the French Surete who eventually located Marty in La Bastide-Saint Pierre. A search of his lodgings uncovered a press, inks, and paper almost identical to the 1000-franc notes. Marty had done his homework well. After his arrest he boasted that with his multiple plates, he could produce a counterfeit which would defy detection. Raymond Marty never had the chance to put his theory into practice.

A CHALLENGE TO A U.S. PATENT

Mrs. Betta Heiland harbored no delusions of power like Emperor Norton, but she did believe she had as much right to issue currency as did the United States Government. "Nobody

It's the first dollar I ever made.

AS SECURE A PRINTING PLANT AS ANYONE WOULD WANT

To enter security areas of institutions where currency is printed requires proper identification and careful monitoring. This institution was no different, except it was not supposed to be printing negotiable paper. This was the Oklahoma State Penitentiary at McAlester.

On April 10, 1927, prison officials conducting a routine search for narcotics, found a cache of 286 counterfeit postal money orders in the printing room of the prison. The imitations were so good that Secret Service, Treasury agents and U.S. Post Office inspectors were called.

Although the printing plate was not found, the seal and dollar signs appeared to be hand cut from a wood block, made by someone who had plenty of time on his hands. There was one tiny clue to the perpetrator's education, or lack of it. The word *continental* was misspelled *continential!*

The package of bogus money orders did not appear newly wrapped. Officials suspected it may have been hidden for many years and that some money orders may have been cashed.

The warden was not sure who made the counterfeits, but suspicion pointed to Frank Hadley, then serving a life term for murder, his second stay at McAlester. He had originally served an eight-year sentence for assault with intent to kill. During his initial incarceration, Hadley had worked for two years in the prison print shop, and upon his return, was placed in charge of the print shop, based on his prior experience.

While no one was ever charged in the case of the McAlester counterfeit

has a patent on the design of United States banknotes," she told Secret Service agents who had apprehended her soliciting printers to make her money. "I have as much right to make them as the Government."

On March 4, 1916, the Secret Service moved in on Mrs. Heiland. She had been under surveillance for some time as she unsuccessfully sought a commercial printing house to publish her brand of currency.

Mrs. Heiland experimented with her designs. Not an admirer of Abraham Lincoln, she substituted his portrait with that of her husband, Theodore, a waiter in a Harlem restaurant, on the face of her five-dollar Federal Reserve notes. Proud of her German heritage, her three-dollar bills carried the Imperial German Coat-of-Arms.

Mrs. Heiland was not prosecuted for competing with the Treasury's monopoly on issuing currency but she did trade her New York City Seventh Avenue address for one at Bellevue Hospital.

money orders, postal inspectors explained, "In the code of these men there is nothing which favors any mercy being shown a "snitcher." A man does not give information many times, for there is no compunction on the part of many of the prisoners to put the tale-bearer out of the way."

Frank Hadley did lose his print shop foremanship and no new specimens of McAlester postal money orders ever surfaced again.

SULLIVAN STREET'S BUREAU OF ENGRAVING AND PRINTING

Mario Milatisi's tavern on New York's Lower East Side, Bleeker Street, was a gathering place for get rich quick schemers, and Milatisi often conspired with his customers. The time was 1915, pre-Prohibition, too early to talk about bootlegging—or was it?

The tavern storeroom housed several barrels of wine and other liquors, and Milatisi often speculated on his savings, if taxes were not paid

on these stores. He knew other barkeeps shared his feelings.

Like all good bartenders, Milatisi listened to complaints and shared some of his own. Patron Joseph Carlisi had a peculiar claim to fame. Twenty years earlier, he and his brother Charles had flooded the country with forged checks. So proficient were the Carlisis in their art that the American Bankers Association hired detectives to track them. On October 3, 1895, the brothers were apprehended. Joseph received a four and one-half year sentence; his brother, a year less. Finishing their terms, the brothers disappeared until 1912, when Charles was arrested for forgery and sentenced to fourteen years.

One of the bank detectives assigned to the Carlisi case had been William Flynn. By 1915, Flynn was head of the Secret Service in New York. Crossing paths with Carlisi, Flynn noticed that he had no visible means of support, yet had ample funds to spend. Flynn put agents on Carlisi's trail which led to a small print shop on Sullivan Street. The printery never operated on

---

A LITTLE DAB WILL DO YOU

County officials in Kirbyville, Texas, reported that a man took a few dabs of green paint to raise the face value of a buck to one million dollars! When cashing his creation, the man advised the teller of the Newton Bank that he wanted to deposit all but $200 which he needed immediately. The U.S. Attorney advised local officials that he would waive Federal charges if the Newton County man were tried for lunacy. Who else but a lunatic would expect to cash a million-dollar bill in Kirbyville during the Depression? The date was November 15, 1934.

Sunday, but September 19, 1915, was an exception. On this Sunday the presses were humming along. Flynn decided it was time to act.

A half dozen agents under Flynn's command surrounded the print shop. When Carlisi emerged, the agents remained hidden, but two officers were motioned to follow him. Around a corner, out of sight of the print shop, they nabbed Carlisi. The package under his arm contained counterfeit revenue stamps, fresh off the shop's Chandler & Price letterpress, designed for Milatisi's use.

With Carlisi in custody, the agents raided the print shop and arrested Alexander Acuti, Francisco Alesandro, and Albert Benesi, as the trio was washing. Their short press run had just produced hundreds of dollars in two-dollar revenue stamps. With all four in custody, Federal agents visited Milatisi's saloon, arresting him for violating the Sullivan law, as well as counterfeiting.

Flynn considered the counterfeiters trial his most important, the first case involving the Government's new revenue stamps. He revealed Carlisi's plan to sell the stamps at half-face—a dollar each. Flynn complimented the counterfeiters—their stamps were excellent facsimiles, capable of fooling revenue inspectors, at a cost of thousands of dollars to the government in lost revenues.

Two-dollar Series
1914 Revenue Stamp

THE CASE OF ELIAS SMITH

In the spring of 1985, the American Numismatic Association received a collection of court documents relating to counterfeiting trials in New York courts between 1820 and 1865. These important papers were the gift of J. Roy Pennell, a founder of the Society of Paper Money Collectors, one of the foremost collectors of currency in the country. Not only were the court documents and depositions included, but specimens of the spurious notes as well. Among the more interesting are the documents relating to the State vs. Elias Smith.

On July 3, 1862, Elias Smith of New York City, tendered a five-dollar bill, purportedly issued by a small mid-central New York bank in Weedsport. He gave the bill to Joseph G. Meeker in payment of a small purchase and accepted other currency in change. Justice was swift in those days, though not always proper. One week later, Elias Smith found himself facing a judge and jury. A. Oakey Hall represented the people. Elias Smith was charged with forgery in the second degree (counterfeiting notes). He pleaded "not guilty."

Although the court documents are without explanation, Smith was granted a continuance. On August 8, 1862, the court allowed him to withdraw his "not guilty" plea. Four days later, the indictment was "discharged" to allow Smith to enlist in the service.

It would be nice to report that Elias Smith went on to heroism in the Civil War, but history does not indicate this. In fact, the records of the Military Service Branch of the National Archives show no enlistment of Elias Smith in the summer of 1862. Three Elias Smiths did serve from New York,

Elias Smith's specimen of the Bank of Weedsport five-dollar note

two prior to our Elias Smith's trial, and the third beginning March 16, 1865, but these were of the wrong period.

Could it be that Elias Smith was an *alias* Smith and conned the court the same as he tried Joseph Meeker?

THE MAN OF MANY NAMES

In June 1837, a group of Michigan businessmen organized the Bank of Ann Arbor on eighty thousand dollars of capitalization. Josiah Childs was named president and the board of directors advertised that the bank was secured for double the amount of currency it would circulate. The New York bank note companies of Rawson, Wright & Hatch and Burton, Gurley & Edmonds designed and printed an elaborate series of currency notes for the new bank in denominations of one-, one-and-one-quarter-, three-, five-, ten- and twenty-dollars. Only one thing remained—a grand opening. It never materialized.

Notes of the Bank of Ann Arbor became counterfeiters' models. Spurious copies eventually flooded commercial channels and tradesmen everywhere were alerted to the Bank of Ann Arbor issues. Few would accept them.

For the rest of his days, James

Brown must have regretted visiting the store of George Rogers, at 14 Carmine Street, New York City, on June 4, 1838. On that morning Brown purchased a breast pin for five dollars and tendered a ten-dollar bill of the Bank of Windham, Connecticut. The bill was worn and torn, but Rogers placed the note in his cash box and gave Brown the pin and five dollars in "good current bills" in change. Rogers suspected the bill had been altered and officials substantiated his suspicions. Originally one of the counterfeits of the Bank of Ann Arbor, the name of the bank, city and state had been carefully scraped from the surface of the bill and WINDHAM added for both the name of the bank and the city of issue. The word CONNECTICUT replaced MICHIGAN on the face.

Only three days earlier, Brown had purchased from Samuel Winterton, items totaling $4.50. He handed Winterton a twenty-dollar bill of the Eagle Bank of Providence, Rhode Island and received appropriate change. The note Brown cashed was genuine, only Brown had applied his penmanship skills to this note, too. He *kited* it—raised the value from two to twenty dollars!

When James Brown was arrested, officials found that he had also applied his penmanship skills to many forms of identification, showing a partiality

Spurious Bank of Ann Arbor note altered to represent Connecticut's Bank of Windham

toward the name Charles. The court obliged, he was indicted as James Brown, alias Charles Randolph, alias Charles Cromwell, alias Charles Forret, alias Charles Chase.

Brown pleaded not guilty and took the Fifth Amendment, a rather uncommon practice then. Inexplicably, the district attorney chose not to try Brown on these charges. Was the man of many aliases tried on more serious charges, or by coincidence was he merely the recipient of many altered notes?

AS PHONY AS A $3 BILL

Numismatists have contributed many slang expressions to the English language—*two bits, sawbuck, fin,*—but not the expression "As phony as a three-dollar bill!" Every collector knows that there were, indeed, three-dollar bills. There were hundreds of different issues including Continental currency, state bank notes, even a United States issue was proposed in 1862. James McKenna saw nothing so unusual about the denomination that it should lead to his arrest and trial on charges of counterfeiting!

February 10, 1820, found James McKenna in New York Court charged that

> "on the fifth day of February in the year of our Lord one thousand eight hundred and twenty—

with force and arms, at the First Ward of the city of New-York, in the county of New-York aforesaid, feloniously had in his custody and possession, and did receive from some person or persons to the jurors aforesaid unknown, a certain false, forged and counterfeited promissory note for the payment of money, commonly called a bank note...."

Counterfeiting was then so common a crime that court documents were preprinted with all the accusatory statements prepared in advance. Only the dates and names of the defendants were left blank and inserted just before trial. In these days before cameras, Court clerks had to have some artistic talent, as they were required to provide an example of the spurious note. McKenna was charged with counterfeiting a three-dollar bill of the Bank of Orange County. He pleaded, "not guilty."

The Bank of Orange County had been incorporated seven years earlier, in 1813, to serve the needs of Goshen, sixty miles northwest of New York City. The period predated the issuance of United States currency; banks issued their own currency and the Bank of Orange County released a complete series, from one-dollar to one-hundred dollars.

A number of witnesses testified that McKenna possessed the spurious bill.

CITY AND COUNTY } ss.
OF NEW-YORK,

The Jurors of the People of the State of New-York, *in and for the Body of the City and County of New-York, upon their Oath,* PRESENT:

THAT *James Mc Kenna* ———— late of the First Ward of the city of New-York, in the county of New-York, aforesaid, *Labourer*

on the *fifth* ——— day of *February* in the year of our Lord one thousand eight hundred and twenty ——— with force and arms, at the First Ward of the city of New-York, in the county of New-York aforesaid, feloniously had in his custody and possession, and did receive from some person or persons to the jurors aforesaid unknown, a certain false, forged and counterfeited promissory note for the payment of money, commonly called a bank note, which said last mentioned false, forged and counterfeited promissory note for the payment of money, is as follows, that is to say,

N° 7421

③ B

The President .... Director & Co
of the Bank of Orange county promise to
pay Three Dollars on demand to J Divine or bearer
Goshen Nov 10 1817
M Robinson & 3 Jr G D Weckman pc

with intention to utter and pass the same, and to permit, cause, and procure the same to be uttered and passed, with the intention to defraud *the President Directors and Company of the Bank of Orange county and other persons to the jurors aforesaid unknown* ——— he the said ×

then and there well knowing the said last mentioned false, forged and counterfeited promissory note for the payment of money, to be false, forged and counterfeited as aforesaid, against the form of the statute in such case made and provided, and against the peace of the people of the state of New-York and their dignity.

And the Jurors aforesaid, upon their Oath aforesaid, do further present, That the said *James Mc Kenna*
afterwards, to wit.
on the said *fifth* ——— day of *February* in the year of our Lord one thousand eight hundred and twenty ——— with force and arms, at the First Ward of the city of New-York, in the county of New-York, aforesaid, feloniously and falsely did utter and publish as true, with intention to defraud, *the said President Directors and Company of the Bank of Orange county and other persons to the jurors aforesaid unknown*

Counterfeiting was so common in the early nineteenth century that charges were preprinted and the names and dates were simply added to the prepared documents

McKenna did not deny that he had handled the bill—he had endorsed it; his name was on the back. The jury examined the bill. But if it were counterfeit, a person with far more talent than a laborer like McKenna had made it. The quality of design and printing matched the other denominations exhibited. There were no telltale marks, no apparent errors, the paper was proper. What made the authorities think the note was counterfeit? It was a three-dollar bill and the Bank of Orange County was not one of the banks issuing this denomination!

The jury looked at the laborer, looked at the bill, and said, "Not guilty!"

Postscript: The Bank of Orange County is one of the oldest, continuously operating banks in the U.S. First opened in 1813, it was changed to the National Bank of Orange County in 1865 and is in operation today.

THE SOUTH SHALL RISE AGAIN

The promotional literature reads, "Very few people throw away an aged banknote. It *looks* genuine—it *smells* genuine—it *feels* genuine." And, to the teller at a downtown Stockholm bank—it *was* genuine!

Impact Specialties Company of Des Plaines, Illinois, is just one of several novelty advertising companies offering parchment reproductions of obsolete currency and a Stockholm bricklayer is just one of several individuals who have concocted ways to cash them in. Ironically, the reproductions neither look, smell, or feel genuine. The original notes were never printed on heavy, oil-soaked parchment. Genuine paper was usually very thin, had a soft feel, and certainly, never smelled!

While Impact Specialties sold its reproductions as attention getters, offering to print advertisers' messages on the reverse, Martin-Cumings Enterprises produced the reproductions in packets for "educational purposes." Packets of Confederate currency, Texas currency, Colonial currency, and New York obsolete currency were available with accompanying histories and descriptions. These packets were offered in novelty stores, by some coin dealers, and in museum stores, including the prestigious Smithsonian Institution. Original buyers were well aware of the fake status of the notes. It was the secondary buyers who were often duped.

Such was the case in the Swedish capital in the mid-1950s. Stockholm's police chief, P.H. Stjernstroem,

Counterfeit three-dollar bill of the Bank of Orange County, used as evidence in the trial of James McKenna

reported that "an unidentified foreigner" was seen in a snow-covered public square giving away "bundles" of Confederate currency. One man received forty bills and others had seen the notes blowing about the streets and parks of Stockholm for weeks. With Impact Specialties selling the copies for as little as twenty-four dollars per thousand, the visitor must have had a field day, but at least one bank teller saw little humor in the free distribution.

Six months after the give-away, an unnamed bricklayer walked into an unnamed bank, explained to a teller that the $500 Confederate bill, dated February 17, 1864, had been given to him by his father, who had inherited it from his father, who had been in the United States before and during the Civil War. Perhaps the teller had heard that "the South Shall Rise Again;" or perhaps the *look, smell,* and *feel* were genuine enough to be convincing. He exchanged the bill for 2,570 kroner!

After police were summoned, Stockholm newspapers were asked to reproduce a copy of the note on their front pages of August 25, 1956. The teller convinced himself that it could happen to anyone. Police were going to see that it did not.

The bricklayer was apprehended—too late. He had spent most of the money and the bank sued for its return.

HELPING THEIR BROTHER CONDUCTORS

Gridlock, the traffic engineer's fear of a complete breakdown of vehicular movement through city streets, was a common occurrence in the early days of the streetcar. Trolley lines hogged the centers of the busiest streets; horse-drawn wagons and early, chain-driven, hard rubber tired trucks, double-parked; pedestrians ignored crosswalks. The situation was chaotic!

By 1911, streetcar conductors had succeeded in reducing their workday from sixteen to twelve hours, but they still took major abuse for traffic jams. Little was done to ease the trolleyman's situation until the Farris brothers, William and John, conductors on the

Confederate States of America $500, payable two years after the ratification of a Treaty of Peace between the Confederate States and the United States. General Stonewall Jackson is on the right and George Washington, astride his horse, is at left within the Confederate seal.

Illinois Central Railroad, devised a scheme.

The Farrises, in partnership with an itinerant printer named Joseph C. Hart, created a successful method of producing thousands of dollars worth of streetcar tickets—all counterfeit. The enterprise was conceived in 1907 when William fell victim to a bait and switch scam: he shelled out $100 for a well-wrapped and sealed bundle of Cleveland Street-railway tickets, worth no more than cut newspaper.

Stung by the swindle and with no one to complain to, Farris decided to make an easy buck. He reasoned that if he bit, others would too, and discussed the plan with this brother and Joe Hart. Pooling their resources, they invested in a small hand-operated printing press. Hart located a can of black printing ink, a supply of paper, copied a single strip of five Cleveland Car Company tickets and made an electroplate. It mattered little that the paper was a little thicker, a shade stiffer. Who would examine every cardboard ticket tendered, except the conductor?

For four years the Farrises and Hart operated a successful scam selling strips of five tickets for six cents to intermediaries who sold the spurious tickets to streetcar conductors for two to three cents per strip profit. The operation braked to an end when the appearance of hundreds of pasteboard tickets, slightly different from the originals, aroused the suspicions of street railway officials.

The railway company engaged detectives to ride the trolley lines, and they shortly witnessed a conductor taking a number of strips from an envelope. He was arrested and confessed to his involvement. The conductor named the source of his phony tickets and the paper trail led to the Farris brothers who, by 1911, were in Chicago planning duplicate scams there and in Columbus and Indianapolis, too.

Raiding the brother's Stony Island Avenue flat near Chicago's lakefront, police discovered the complete printing plant in their kitchen. In addition to the small press, they seized plates for fare tickets of several cities, including 90,000 packaged for delivery to Cleveland. Many a conductor had doubled his weekly income with the help of the Farris brothers and their printing press.

STRETCHING IT A BIT TOO FAR

Captain William H. Houghton sat at his desk in the Secret Service headquarters, Philadelphia, studying an imitation dollar bill that had passed as genuine.

He shook his head in disbelief that anyone could have accepted the bill, a rubber buck printed for and sold in novelty stores throughout the city. Nevertheless, the Secret Service chief was aware of regulations. Houghton dispatched a squad of agents to make raids on all magic and novelty stores, and seize any printing plates or specimens of the stretchable dollars.

Houghton's order proved very unpopular with his agents. Regulations require confiscated items to be destroyed in the small furnace in the office by burning one at a time, properly observed, properly witnessed—paper, or rubber was immaterial!

THE GREEN CHICKEN STORE MONEY

Grocery store coupons are a secondary currency in the United States. They are bought, sold, traded, even counterfeited. Although their cash value is a fraction of a cent, the purchasing power is great. Usually the discounts off the retail prices average ten to fifteen percent.

Figures show a potential of more than a hundred billion coupons with a face value of twenty billion circulating in 1986. With that potential, entrepreneurs naturally want a piece of the action. Some pass coupons at the checkout stand without purchasing the product. But others make it a big operation.

Norman Towne, a California accountant, started in coupons in a big way. His confederates were housewives duped into clipping newspaper coupons for charity, and paid by the pound. He was redeeming his millions of coupons at the rate of $300,000 per month when apprehended. In November 1978, Towne was tried, convicted, sentenced to two years imprisonment, and fined $8,000 in real greenbacks, a sentence harsher than for many who were caught printing Uncle Sam's primary currency.

A few years ago the Postal Service, in attempting to crack down on fraudulent practices with coupons, published a bogus one in a New York newspaper. It appeared only one time but within weeks, more than 2,000 retailers in forty states tried to redeem copies of the dummy coupon!

Some newspapers use the secondary currency to promote circulation. Their front pages boast the total retail value of the coupons printed inside, and many a thrifty housewife is willing to pay fifteen cents for another issue of the newspaper containing five to six dollars worth of coupons. Grocers themselves are not always clean; they often purchase unsold newspapers, clip the coupons and deduct the amount from invoices. They also receive a five- to ten-cent "handling charge" to reimburse them for additional work at checkout stands. Even worse are the "green chicken" stores, operated only for the large scale redemption of the secondary currency. Via the coupon route, moldy foods are, indeed turned into genuine greenbacks.

An estimated $315 million in coupons are fraudulently redeemed each year

AFTERSTORIES

THE MONEY DESIGNED TO SAVE LIVES

London in the early nineteenth century is a time of scant entertainment—the government charges Sunday visitors to Bethlehem Hospital (better known as Bedlam) a shilling to watch the helpless antics of the mentally ill. Public executions are also prime entertainment. The victim of a hangman's rope must tip the executioner to insure that the rope is tied properly and death is not prolonged. For added insurance, the victim invites his friends. They can pull on his legs should the executioner get carried away with entertaining the public too long. This is "The Age of Enlightenment."

George Cruikshank, born in London in 1792 and now scarcely out of his teens, is a leading illustrator of his day. His caricatures are troubled editorials and he is equally comfortable attacking the Tories, the Whigs, or the Radicals, but perhaps best known for his Oliver Twist. A contemporary biographer says

"He works with fine impartiality—satirical capital comes to him from every public event—wars abroad, the enemies of England (Cruikshank is very patriotic), the camp, the court, the senate, the church; low life, high life; the humours of the people and the follies of the great."

Cruikshank himself tells of one of his far reaching campaigns.

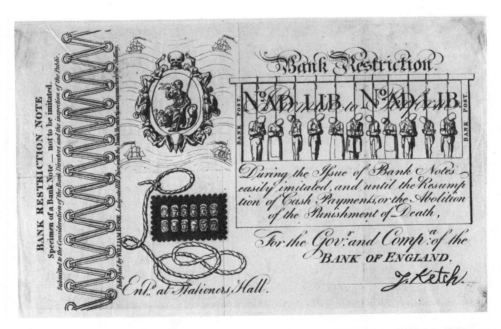

Specimen of the "Bank Note—Not to be Imitated." This satirical currency note spelled the end of one-pound notes and brought an end to hanging for forgery

HOW I PUT A STOP TO HANGING

"It is now the year 1817, there are one-pound Bank of England notes in circulation, and, unfortunately, there are forged one-pound notes in circulation also; and the punishment for passing these forged notes is in some cases transportation for life (to Australia), in others, DEATH!

"Presently, I reside in Dorset-Street, Salisbury Square, Fleet Street, and had occasion to go early this morning to a house near the Bank of England, and in returning home between eight and nine o'clock down Ludgate Hill, and seeing a number of persons looking up Old Bailey, I look that way myself, and see several human beings hanging on the gibbet opposite Newgate prison, and to my horror two of these are WOMEN; and, upon inquiring what these women are being hung for, am informed that it is for passing forged one-pound notes. The fact that a poor woman could be put to death for such a minor offense has a great effect upon me—and I at the moment determine, if possible, to put a stop to this shocking destruction of life, for merely obtaining a few shillings by fraud, and well knowing the habits of the low classes of society in London, I feel quite sure that in very many cases the rascals who forge these notes induce these poor ignorant women to go into the gin-shops to 'get something to drink,' and thus pass the notes, and hand them the change.

"My residence is a short distance from Ludgate Hill, and after witnessing this tragic scene I return home, and in ten minutes design and make a sketch of this 'Bank note not to be imitated.' Half an hour after this is done, William Home (my publisher) comes into my room and sees the sketch lying upon my table; he is much struck with it and says, 'What are you going to do with this, George?' 'To publish it,' I reply. Then he says, 'Will you let me have it?' To his request I consent, make an etching of it, and it is published. Mr. Home resides on Ludgate Hill, not many yards from the spot where I had seen the people hanging on the gibbet, and when it appears in his shop window it creates a great sensation, and the people gather round his house in such numbers that the lord mayor sends the city police to disperse the crowd. The bank directors hold a meeting immediately upon the subject, and AFTER THAT they issue no more one-pound notes, and so there is no more hanging for passing FORGED one-pound notes; not only that, but ultimately no hanging, even for forgery. AFTER THIS Sir Robert Peel passes a bill in Parliament for the 'Resumption of cash payments.' AFTER THIS he revises the penal code, and AFTER THAT there are not any more hangings or punishment of DEATH for minor offenses.

"In a work that I am preparing for publication I intend to give a copy of 'The Bank Note,' as I consider it the most important design and etching that I have made in my life; for it will save the lives of thousands of my fellow creatures, and for having been able to do this Christian act I am most sincerely thankful."

George Cruikshank

Author's Notes:

1. Cruikshank's comments are adapted from a letter written by him and published in the Gloucester Journal in 1876, two years before he died.

2. The Bank of England's one-pound notes indeed disappeared from circulation. Although specimen one-pound notes were made in 1902, the denomination was not reintroduced into circulation until just before World War I, almost a century later. The new designs required expert engraving skills, so were less likely to be imitated. Cruikshank's concerns over the simplicity of design and the temptation to counterfeit brought an end to public hangings in England.

THE START OF SOMETHING BIG

The art of counterfeiting began shortly after the first coin changed hands in the marketplace of Lydia in 660 B.C. Today counterfeiters cost merchants millions of dollars and an equal amount is spent tracking them. Authenticators for the American Numismatic Association Certification Service (ANACS) headquartered in Colorado Springs, Colorado study such practices as date alteration and rare coin reproduction. Had it not been for a band of counterfeiters, a young barrel maker might not have become one of the world's great detectives, and the United States would have been without the services of its largest private detective agency, a name synonymous with private guard service—Pinkerton!

A counterfeit one-pound note dated 1818. The spurious bill was as crude as the genuine.

Allan Pinkerton

Allan Pinkerton was like most Scots of his time: frugal, honest, often curious, but not the least prosperous. He was politically outspoken, especially on matters involving the British crown. Pinkerton fled his native Scotland one step ahead of process servers. His call to reform the British Parliament had been too loud. His words reached the ears of the English overlords and his arrest was ordered.

The year was 1842. Pinkerton headed as far from British jurisdiction as possible, to Dundee in the wooded suburbs of Chicago, an area being settled by many Scots.

The young Highlander continued the only trade he knew—coopering, the making of barrels—procuring raw materials from nature, not from the woodworking shops of Dundee or Chicago. On one of his forays to a small island in a river near his home, Pinkerton's Scot curiousity was aroused. Finding embers of a recent campfire, unlike those set by woods-men or passing transients, Pinkerton's intuitiveness convinced him something illicit had occurred. Several times he returned to observe the campsite and late one evening his perseverance was rewarded—he spotted a small group of men working quietly over a new fire. Hurrying back to Dundee, he told his story to the sheriff and together they returned. Taken by surprise, the men quickly surrendered and the sheriff confiscated all the paraphernalia needed to make pass-cast copies of United States coins.

Allan Pinkerton became a local hero. When a flood of counterfeit notes of the Wisconsin Marine & Fire Insurance Company plagued local merchants, they turned to Pinkerton to find the source. Allan Pinkerton found his man and became the first full-time detective for the Chicago Police Department. Two years later, he started his own private detective agency. Thousands of security guards today owe their employment to that small band of woodland counterfeiters.

SOPHISTICATED EQUIPMENT COMBATS THE FORGER'S ART

Edward J. Fleischmann has a job not unlike one at Mission Control in Houston. He sits behind a huge electronic console monitoring a TV screen as it scans an arid, moonlike surface complete with ridges and valleys, craters small and large, fissures and surface cracks. He adjusts countless knobs and dials to enhance the image or to magnify a particular point of interest.

Fleischmann is not viewing a distant planet for signs of life. He is inspecting the magnified surface of a coin for signs of alteration or forgery. Fleisch-

Ed Fleischmann at "Mission Control"

mann is an authenticator for ANACS, the certification service of the American Numismatic Association.

With the values of many coins in the thousands of dollars, coin forgery and coin alteration has become a big business. ANACS examines an average of 7,500 coins per month, up from 3,000 in just one year. The forger's art has become so sophisticated that methods to detect and expose forgeries must be more technical; mere weighing and studied opinions are no longer sufficient. ANACS employs a scanning electron microscope (SEM) capable of enlargements to one-half million times actual size. At 700 times actual size, surface lines caused by flowing metal filling cavities of the dies during the striking process, become clues to the coin's authenticity. Forgers are imitating these flowlines even though the lines are microscopic.

Ever since collectors started paying premiums for 1916-D Mercury dimes, forgers have been busy altering the more common Philadelphia Mint variety, for sale to unwary collectors.

At present, a 1916 dime in good condition retails for $2.75; the same date and condition struck at the Denver Mint lists for $275. Uncirculated, the differential is even greater—$32 vs. $2,850.

At first, forgers simply chiseled a D mintmark from a later issue common coin and glued it to the surface of a Philadelphia issue. When some marks actually fell off in coin holders used to display them, forgers tried drilling a hole partially through from the other side and punching a "D" through the thinned surface from the reverse of the coin. Now collectors had to examine both sides of the coin for alteration. Recent epoxies allow the forger to again cement "D" mintmarks to the surface without fear of separation.

At least one forger has gone one step further. A recent SEM examination of a 1916-D dime purchased from a reputable dealer, underscored the forger's sophistication. The flowlines had been hand-tooled onto the edges of the mintmark to hide its addition to the surface of the coin. Flowlines radiate out from the center toward the edge of the coin, which the forger could not quite imitate. A few of the mintmark lines were at right angles to those on the surface, an indication that the "D" had been added to this Mercury dime.

When such discrepancies occur, a second TV monitor is attached to the electron microscope. The video projects an image on to a sheet of photographic film, making it permanent for further study and for evidence should the forger be apprehended. A complete inventory of all known counterfeit and altered coins is maintained by ANACS in Colorado Springs.

PROFESSOR NICHOLS' CAVEAT

A.A. Smith, professor emeritus at North-Western College, prepared an introduction for *The Business Guide* or *Safe Methods of Business*, authored by his colleague and friend, J.L. Nichols, principal of the Naperville, Illinois, business school. Professor Smith recommended the book

"to all who desire, in a cheap form, full information as to methods of doing business...for lack of that information which this book contains, business men lose thousands of dollars every day. Millions are lost in litigation, owing to careless habits, or to ignorance of the proper methods of doing business, to say nothing of the losses, for the same reason, by the trickery of confidence-men and sharpers in general."

The year was 1886, when many gave thought to a quick buck, real or otherwise.

OPPOSITE: From the chapter on common swindles

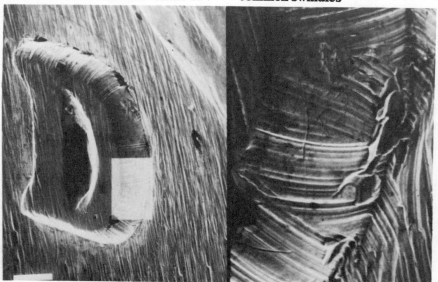

The mintmark added to a 1916-D dime went undetected at first, but magnifying the sloping side of the tiny letter

500 times, showed it to be an addition after the coin left the mint

COUNTERFEIT MONEY SWINDLE.

This scheme has long been practised in different parts of the country, yet the victims are numerous, hundreds being added annually to the list.

It is simply a shrewd system of black-mailing, and worked as follows: The swindlers or black-mailers (as they can more properly be called) get together, make up plausible circulars, and secure advertisements in local newspapers in the territory which they intend to work up. No work is done in their own neighborhood, all operations being planned from headquarters when the victims are selected. The "gang" has a number of schemes, but the favorite one, is to send some person who has answered their circulars, a genuine new bill, and to get him on pretense, to see if it is good. As the bill is genuine there is no difficulty in passing it. The dupe is then informed that he will be supplied with any amount of similar good money at a trifling cost.

If the man bites the tempting bait placed before him, he is made to sign a document which he is told admits him to membership in a secret society known as the Y. F. A. R., and the money is to come in a few days. Instead, however, a man makes his appearance who represents himself as a United States officer; he shows up the document signed by the poor fellow, which practically proves to be a confession of circulating counterfeit money, and also calls his attention to the bill which he passed.

The victim is told that he must go to Washington and be tried by a United States Court, and the penalty for making and passing counterfeit money is also read. He is cleverly told the long delay at heavy cost and the sure penalty.

When the victim is sufficiently wrought up, the officer offers to compromise for all the way from $200 to $2000. The money is paid or secured, the document torn up and the dupe released.

NOTE.—*A man who is caught in a swindling scheme of this kind is utterly helpless and at the mercy of his captors. He dare not go to officers and make complaint against the rascals without exposing himself, because he would never have been caught in the trap had he not shown a willingness to handle and pass counterfeit money, and consequently is as guilty as the swindler in the eyes of the law.*

BEWARE OF STRANGERS WHO OFFER YOU GREAT INDUCEMENTS. BEWARE, BEWARE, BEWARE.

DO GOOD—MAKE GOOD

Prisons are indeed communities, with their own heads of state, police, and laws; population exceeds 350,000 in state and federal prisons at most times. All prisons have their own cultures, their own industries, and many have their own money!

A convict may lose his identity, his self-respect, his right to vote, his freedom from harsh discipline, but he is permitted personal funds to shop in the prison commissary for tobacco, candy, toothpaste, pens, pencils, stationery, etc. which he must buy with his own funds.

One source of income is through prison work programs. The laundries of the 1930s tough-guy movies, the license plate stamping shops, still exist. Convicts may also sell arts and crafts in prison visitor shops, with income credited to the prisoners' personal accounts. Paper credits and debits are preferred to real money, since the latter often leads to bribery and further crime.

Prison money used in the United States has been as varied as the institutions themselves. At Alcatraz, with no commissary facilities, prisoners could order approved items from the outside, to be charged against their accounts. Leavenworth used coupon books, containing pages of various denomination coupons that could be torn out and spent as money. San Quentin initiated punch cards in 1935, with a face value of one dollar. Each card had room for twenty punches—at five cents each. New York's Sing Sing Prison once printed its own paper money and used its own token coinage for change.

In 1915, Sing Sing was wardened by a strict believer in prisons as bastions of protection for society from criminals who simply needed the proper training before being returned to useful citizenship. Thomas Mott Osborne initiated a system of inmate self-government. His "Mutual Welfare League" administration created a currency echoing his motto—*Do Good—Make Good*.

The paper money was issued in denominations of one-, five-, and ten-dollar bills and change tokens in values to match coins circulating on the "outside"—one, five, ten, twenty-five, and fifty cents. Even the size and color of these coins matched—bronze colored brass for the one-cent pieces and silver colored aluminum for the other denominations.

Prison money is not easy to attain, given its limited circulation. Most remains behind when a felon leaves prison, for the money of one "state" is not good in another.

A Sing Sing nickel—The reverse of this five-cent-sized token carries the initials of Thomas Mott Osborne's idealized experiment—the Mutual Welfare League, an inmate self-government system that even issued money

DON'T TAKE ANY WOODEN NICKELS!

"Don't take any wooden nickels!" Have you ever wondered where the expression originated? Etymologists cannot agree. The *Dictionary of American Slang* says the expression means goodbye, take care of your self; protect yourself from trouble; or, don't take any worthless money, attributed to a 1920s fad. William and Mary Morris' *Dictionary of Word and Phrase Origins* skirts the date issue, saying,

"just who first used the expression is not known, but it certainly was a long time ago. The United States minted five-cent pieces from the earliest days of the Union, but they were not known as nickels until 1866, because that was the year the first five-cent coins containing nickel were minted."

The first wooden nickels were called Stamp Money

Numismatists differ with both sources. The first U.S. coin referred to as a "nickel" was not a five-cent piece, but the flying eagle and early Indian head cents. Introduced to general circulation in 1857, the flying eagle cent was twelve percent nickel and whitish in color. In 1859, the first Indian head cents were introduced and until 1864 these, too, were struck in copper-nickel and whitish in appearance.

During this period, half-dimes or silver five-cent pieces were in circulation. In 1866, the Treasury introduced the first five-cent nickel coin, and until 1873, both silver half-dimes and nickel five-cent pieces were produced. To differentiate between the two, citizens started calling them "five-cent silver" and "five-cent nickel." After half-dimes were discontinued, the coins disappeared from circulation and the public shortened the name of the new five-cent piece to "nickel." But that does not explain "wooden nickel."

KEEP THIS STAMP BUSY MAKING CHANGE

1 9 3 3

Stamp 2 CENTS 2 Money

AS IT CIRCULATES IN TENINO IT HELPS

ISSUED TO MEET A SHORTAGE OF CHANGE
BY THE
Thurston County Independent
Tenino, Washington
AND IS RECEIVABLE AT DOUBLE FACE
VALUE ON SUBSCRIPTION PAYMENTS

$1.50 a Year   5 Cents a Copy

The first "official" issue of wooden nickels was in Tenino, Washington, a town known for being original. In discussing a name for their town, early settlers noted that it was situated 1090 feet above sea level. And, that is what they named the town— ten-nine-oh.

In December 1931, three weeks before Christmas Eve, the Citizens Bank of Tenino failed. Residents found themselves without cash and a domino reaction faced many businesses. The local Chamber of Commerce came to the rescue with the first issue of wooden money in the U.S. Using assignments of up to twenty-five percent of the funds on deposit, the Chamber issued scrip for redemption when assets held in the closed bank were released.

The first issues were printed on paper, but later ones were made of thin wooden laminated sheets, with an uncancelled stamp between the sheets to give the money government backing. Publishers of the *Thurston County Independent* printed the money. Various values, shapes and sizes, were issued for the next four years, until the United States Treasury stepped in and ordered: "Don't Take Any Wooden Nickels!"

YOU CAN HAVE ANY COLOR YOU WANT...AS LONG AS IT'S GREEN!

The money of tomorrow—what should it look like? To answer that question took thirty-one million dollars of Government experimentation. First, denominational color, as in most modern nations' paper money, was suggested. Metallic or plastic threads were considered. The ultimate idea was an optical variable device printed on U.S. currency which would change color or shift position when the note was moved from side to side. The new currency was to be the Treasury's answer to sophisticated color copiers that could conceivably turn any modern office into a counterfeiting plant.

Thirty-one million dollars later, Congress has informed the Secretary of the Treasury that he can have any color currency he wants, as long as it's green! Old habits run deep, and it now appears that the world's most counterfeited currency will stay that way a little longer.

Legislation prohibiting the Treasury Department from making major changes in the U.S. currency without approval of Congress was passed unanimously by the House of Representatives. Called the Currency Design Act (HR 48), the bill was introduced after an announced Bureau of Engraving and Printing study to consider changing the design of U.S. currency, to make it more difficult to counterfeit.

HR 48 requires the Treasury to wait ninety days after announcement before implementing any new design. Congress may accept or reject the proposed changes, but if it does not act within the ninety-day period, the new currency may go into production automatically. One suggested change was to print the traditional "greenbacks" in different colors. "Although the Treasury Department says it has abandoned plans to change the color of money," said Rep. Frank Annunzio, sponsor of the bill, "my bill will make certain that the Treasury will follow through on its promise."

Congress has not decided to make life easier for counterfeiters. Rather, said Annunzio, "We want to make certain that a problem exists before any more taxpayers' money is wasted. Eighty million dollars in counterfeit money was seized, and only seven million made its way into the banking system. If the government has already spent thirty-one million and cannot find a solution, how much more money must be spent on the solution to the problem? I want to make certain that the Treasury does not produce another Susan B. Anthony dollar or a two-dollar bill fiasco," he added.

The Bureau of Engraving and Printing is implementing two new changes in the currency, with the Federal Reserve notes, series 1987. Visible to the naked eye, a polyester thread will run vertically through the bill. Printed on the threads will be the denomination, e.g., on the one-, five-, and ten-dollar bills will be the words USAONE, USAFIVE, and USATEN, continuously repeated and visible only when held to the light. The higher denominations, because of space, will read USA20, USA50 and USA100. The threads will run between the left edge and the Federal Reserve Bank seal on all notes except the $1. On this note the thread will appear between the seal and the portrait. The printing will appear only on the face of the notes, but the thread itself will be visible on the back.

The actual designs of the notes will not change, but engraved on the plates, surrounding the portraits will be UNITED STATES OF AMERICA. The legends appearing on the new threads and around the portrait will not copy on ordinary office copiers.

GLOSSARY

THE LANGUAGE OF THE COUNTERFEITER

Every group has its own language or jargon. Counterfeiters are no exception and some of their slang appears below. The listing is not complete, as the lingo of the coin counterfeiter is passe. With inflation, there is no profit in the manufacture of bad coin, unless it is made with the collector in mind. The faking of rare coin for its numismatic value remains a problem, and with the advent of sophisticated copy machines, has come an increase in the clandestine manufacture of United States currency. U.S. paper money is, in fact, the world's most counterfeited currency.

COIN

Counterfeiter:
  caster   coniacker   koniacker   minter

Passer:
  ringer

Product:

cluck	heavy	plug
hard	heavy money	seal
hard money	lead	slug
hard stuff	light piece	stuff
hardware	(small coin)	

Plant:
  mint   money mill

Alter:
  clorox job - dipping a coin in solvent or bleach to clean
  double head - a coin with two heads used in "matching"
  oven job - artificial toning to enhance value
  plug a nickel - add weight to a vending machine token
  raise - impress a mintmark from behind or through the edge
  silver - to plate a cent to look like a dime
  sweat - two halves from a high denomination sweated to two halves of a lower denomination
  whiz - mechanical wire brushing of a coin to make it look uncirculated

CURRENCY

Counterfeiter:

faker   green-goods merchant   green-goods man
queer maker

Plate maker (engraver):

scratcher   scribe

Passing:

bill posting   laying   shoving
hanging paper   pushing   slushing

Many of the terms used for passing bad paper are synonymous with those used for passing bad checks.

Product:

bad dough	bun	gyp	shuffle
blind	dead dollars	queer	slide
*bogus	dud dollars	queer jack	sour
bull-wool	flash	scratch	sour dough

Counterfeiting:

green-goods game   lie on a green back   make the queer

Alter:

flying a kite - to raise a bill by changing the numerals; practiced during the time
of private bank issues

kiting - same as above

nipping - cutting and pasting numerals on a bill to raise the value

*Bogus is also a term given to the machines sold to make counterfeit currency.
(See "The Chicago Money Machine Caper")*

TABLES
LIST OF COMMON REPLICA NOTES

Serial#

Alabama/State of, Montgomery, $100, Jan. 1, 1864 834
Arkansas/Treasury Warrant, $1, April 28, 1862 128346
California/Wells Fargo, San Francisco, $20, Jan. 11, 1871 370455
Canada/City Bank, Montreal, $4, Jan. 1, 1857 12549
Confederate States

    $1, Feb. 17, 1864 82129
    $2, April 6, 1863 46695
    $5, Feb. 17, 1864 18262
    $10, Sept. 2, 1861 5089
    $10, Feb. 17, 1864 40679
    $20, Sept. 2, 1861 1524
    $20, Feb. 17, 1864 46410
    $20, unreadable date - probably Sept. 2, 1861 15247
    $50, Sept. 2, 1861 18443
    $50, Sept. 2, 1861 23961
    $50, April 6, 1863 3987
    $50, Feb. 17, 1864 5670
    $50, Feb. 17, 1864 72104
    $100, May 8, 1862 ....108?
    $100, Nov. 20, 1862 65798
    $100, Nov. 20, 1862 ....no number
    $500, Feb. 17, 1864 16760
    $500, Feb. 17, 1864 18278
    $1,000, May 28, 1861 ....178A
    $1,000, May 28, 1861 ....197A
    $100,000, July 25, 1861 4832

Connecticut

    Colonial, 10 shillings, June 1, 1780 11259
    Bank of New England, uncut sheet $3-5-10-20 unissued ....no

Continental Currency
    Colonial, $20, Sept. 26, 1778 270350

Delaware/Colonial, 5 shillings, Jan. 1, 1776 62101

Florida

    Bank of Fernandia, $5, Feb. 1, 1860 237
    Bank of St. John's, $5, May 2, 1859 667
    Bank of Florida (Tallahassee), $4, Feb. 1, 1864 542
    Bank of West Florida, $10, Nov. 3, 1832 1363

Merchants & Planters Bank, $20, Nov. 12, 1833 ....13??
State of Florida (Tallahassee), $1, Mar. 1, 1863 2396

Georgia
Colonial, $4, Sept. 10, 1777 ....????
Colonial, $4, Sept. 10, 1777 19567
$100, April 6, 1864 ....19567(?)

Indiana
Citizens Banking House, Gosport, $2, July 1, 1857 ....????
Citizens Banking House, Gosport, $3, July 1, 1857 2929
Citizens Banking House, Gosport, $5, July 1, 1857 2658
Exchange Banking House, Indianapolis, $3, Oct. 27, 1819 ....no

Louisiana
Canal Bank, New Orleans, uncut sheet, $10-10-10-10 ....no
Canal Bank, New Orleans, uncut sheet, $10-20-20-20 ....no
Canal Bank, New Orleans, uncut sheet, $100-100-100-100 ....no
State of Louisiana, $100, March 10, 1863 2650

Maryland
Colonial, $8, April 10, 1774 14020
Somerset & Worcester Savings Bank, $2, Nov. 1, 1862 1564

Massachusetts/Colonial, $8, May 5, 1780 25480

Michigan
Macomb County Bank, $2, April 1, 1758 5203
Tecumseh Bank, $1, undated ....no

Mississippi/Treasury note, $100, Jan. 8, 1862 2758

New Hampshire
Colonial, 30 shillings, Aug. 24, 1778 992
Colonial, $7, April 29, 1870 ....1702 or A702

New Jersey
Colonial, 18 pence, March 25, 1775 8418
Union County Bank, Plainfield, $5, Sept. 12, 1859 ....no

New York
Colonial, 5 pounds, Feb. 16, 1771 24323
Colonial, $10, Aug. 13, 1776 ....unreadable no.
Bulls Head Bank, New York City, $3, Aug. 10, 1864 4042
Clinton Bank, $100, Dec. 2, 1839 9

City Trust & Banking Co. $2,000,000, Dec. 21, 1839 5509
Corporation of the City of Albany, 10 cents, July 17, 1862 676
Genessee County Bank, $52.12, May 5, 1865 16896
Sherman & Barnes, Buffalo, 25 cents, July 11, 1862 ....no

North America
Bank of Philadelphia, $1, Jan. 30, 1862 28
Bank of Philadelphia, $1,000, Jan. 30, 1862 22

North Carolina
Colonial, $4, Aug. 8, 1778 ....126 or 146
State of North Carolina, $1, Sept. 1, 1862 808

Ohio
Bank of Granville, $3, May 11, 1838 7374
State Bank of Ohio, Franklin Center Branch, Columbus, $1,
July 7, 1861 9131

Pennsylvania/Colonial, 15 shillings, Oct. 1, 1773 5520

Rhode Island/Colonial, $3, July 2, 1780 2298

South Carolina
Colonial, 5 shillings, April 10, 1778 640
Colonial, $8, Oct. 19, 1776 ....no
Cotton Planters Loan Association, $5, May 15, 1862 415

Tennessee/Bank of Chattanooga, $2, Jan. 4, 1863 ....no

Texas
Republic of, $1, June 10, 1840 2150
Republic of, $2, March 1, 1841 5214
Republic of, $3, Sept. 1, 1841 383
Republic of, $5, Jan. 15, 1842 2231
Republic of, $10, Jan. 25, 184? 5480
Republic of, $20, Jan. 10, 1840 1575
Republic of, $50, Jan. 1, 1840 1112
Republic of, $100, 1839 ....15?
Republic of, $100, May 29, 1839 663
Republic of, $500, Jan. 1, 1840 1381
Texas Treasury Warrant, $5, Oct. 6, 1862 112586
United States
Bank of, Washington, $10, Jan. 23, 1834 646
Bank of, Washington, $1,000, Dec. 15, 1840 8894
Bank of, Washington, $1,000,000, Dec. 25, 1840
Payable to Daniel Boone 711

Print the next one upside down, we'll be rich!

PICTURE CREDITS

INDEX

ABOUT THE AUTHOR

As a professional numismatist, Ed Rochette has spent a lifetime actively engaged in the hobby of coin collecting on a full-time basis. Joining the staff of Krause Publications in 1960, as editor of *Numismatic News,* he published the first of more than 1,000 articles on coins and coin collecting. Six years later, Rochette was named editor of *The Numismatist,* the official journal of the American Numismatic Association. In 1972, he was named the association's chief executive officer. Today, he heads his own consulting firm specializing in association management, development and fund raising.

Recognition as a hobby leader has been noted in many ways:

● Appointed to the United States Assay Commission by President Lyndon Johnson in 1965.

● Member of three-person panel to select official U.S. Bicentennial Medal.

● Advisory panel, General Services Administration, for the disposal of surplus silver dollars.

● American delegate to the Federation Internationale de la Medaille Conference, Stockholm, Sweden.

● Leader, State Department endorsed People-to-People Goodwill Tour of Eastern Europe.

● Recipient, American Numismatic Association's Medal of Merit.

● Advisor, Numismatics, Roosevelt University

● Established and supervised American Numismatic Association Summer Seminar classes, Colorado College, now in their eighteenth year.

As a professional writer, Ed Rochette's articles have appeared in most hobby publications. He has earned the Numismatic Literary Guild's honors for Best Feature Writer and Best Syndicated Column. His *Coin Roundup* appears in many major newspapers, including the prestigious *Newsday, Baltimore Sun* and *Chicago Sun-Times.* His book, *Medallic Portraits of John F. Kennedy* is a standard reference for collectors and earned him the coveted Token and Medal Society's Sandra Rae Mishler Gold Medal for original research. His travels to 26 different countries and tours of more than 40 government and private mints serves as the genesis for many feature articles and lectures.